Ministry of Reconciliation

Ministry
of
Reconciliation

Modern Lessons
from Scripture and Sacrament

David W. Barry

ALBA · HOUSE  NEW · YORK

SOCIETY OF ST. PAUL, 2187 VICTORY BLVD., STATEN ISLAND, NEW YORK 10314

Library of Congress Cataloging in Publication Data

Barry, David W.
Ministry of reconciliation.

Includes bibliographical references.
1.   Penance.   I.   Title.
BX2260.B28   265'.6   75-4630
ISBN   0-8189-0317-1

Nihil Obstat:
J. Robert Yeazel
Censor Librorum
Imprimatur:
+ David F. Cunningham
Bishop of Syracuse
December 3, 1974

The Nihil Obstat and Imprimatur
are a declaration that a book or pamphlet is considered
to be free from doctrinal or moral error. It is not implied that
those who have granted the Nihil Obstat and Imprimatur agree
with the contents, opinions or statements expressed.

Designed, printed and bound in the United States of
America by the Fathers and Brothers of the Society of St. Paul,
2187 Victory Boulevard, Staten Island, New York, 10314,
as part of their communications apostolate.

1 2 3 4 5 6 7 8 9 (Current Printing: first digit).

ACKNOWLEDGEMENTS

For contributions to this writer which bear fruit in these pages, I acknowledge and sincerely thank:

Mrs. Elizabeth Angelino, Oneida, N.Y.; Rev. Joseph D. Barry, C.S.C., Akron, Ohio; Sister Agnes Rose Burton, C.S.J. Albany, N.Y.; Rev. Joseph M. Champlin, Fulton, N.Y.; Dr. Edward J. Cronin, University of Notre Dame; Rev. John S. Dunne, C.S.C., University of Notre Dame; Dr. James J. Hillenbrand, Oneida, N.Y.; Sister Anne Lehner, S.S.S., Syracuse, N.Y.; Rev. Patrick J. Logan, St. Bernard's Seminary, Rochester, N.Y.; Rev. William D. Lum, Rochester, N.Y.; Rev. Richard L. Osborne, Syracuse, N.Y.; Mr. William J. Ryan, Syracuse, N.Y.; Rev. Richard S. Sturtz, Wadhams Hall Seminary, Ogdensburg, N.Y.; Rev. John P. Wagner, Rev. J. Robert Yeazel, Syracuse, N.Y.

Scripture quotations taken from *The Jerusalem Bible* (Doubleday & Co., Inc.) and *The New American Bible* (P. J. Kenedy & Sons) translations.

CONTENTS

AUTHOR'S PREFACE

I can offer two observations as an apologia for this book. First, as a parish priest it is clear to me that the post Vatican II parish community—with its quandries, anxieties, and general fluidity of attitudes about the Church—looks to its priests and religious educators for an approach to modern faith-reality that "makes sense." To the layman, I believe, this means that counseling, sermons, and personal spirituality they find in their religious leaders a self-possessed consistency that bespeaks a reverence for what has brought us this far—and an enlightened enthusiasm for the forces of the Spirit that are shaping the future.

My second observation—in line with Pope Paul's call for the 1975 Holy Year of Reconciliation—is that *spiritual integrity* (a sense of unifying wholeness about one's life in faith) constitutes that kind of "interior renewal" badly needed by so many today. The present adult generation of believers finds it difficult to cope with the "changes in the Church," largely, I feel, because much of their education in faith-matters has been halting or stultified. They have been forced to memorize too much and "think through" too little; to "hear" Mass rather than participate in liturgy; to "avoid sin" but not always to cultivate virtue; to revere rubric and precept, while gaining little exposure to understanding the celebration of rites or conscience primacy.

I would like to feel that in some way this book might contribute to the overall theme of reconciliation abroad in the Church today. Proximately this means dealing with the nature of sin as fragmentation, and of the renewal of Penance as Sacrament of healing and restoration to wholeness.

On a more general level my intention has been to apply "reconciliation" to the *faith experience*: drawing out the lesson that there is inherent unity and an even-flowing concordance to what Gospel reveals, Church teaches, liturgy celebrates, and Christian responsibility demands. To be thus "reconciled" is to enjoy the "life more abundantly."

David W. Barry
Syracuse, New York

If anyone is in Christ, he is a new creation. The old order has passed away; now all is new! All this has been done by God, who has reconciled us to himself through Christ and has given us the ministry of reconciliation.

2 Corinthians 5:17-18

Chapter I

Unless A Man Be Born Again

In spite of their undeserved reputation as unemotional automatons, many of America's 32 space travelers have been profoundly moved by their experiences away from earth. In some cases, they have returned to begin entirely different lives.

—*Time* magazine
December 11, 1972

The long-awaited age of American manned spaceflight broke with the dawn of May 5, 1961 over the reclaimed swamplands of southern Florida. The quarter-hour "joyride" of Commander Alan B. Shepard downrange from Cape Canaveral aboard the first of the manned Mercury space capsules christened a revolutionary moment in human experience as well as in scientific history. For, significant as they have been, the fascinating discoveries resulting from our spaceflight programs have exceeded even the now-broadened limits of the purely scientific and technological.

What scientists call "spin-off phenomena"—unanticipated results of observation or experiment—have surfaced in the attitudinal and behavioral changes evident in some of the astronauts since their spaceflight missions. While peering back at their native planet—and viewing it in all the delicate totality a glimpse from tens of thousands of miles in space affords—several of these men have reported similar sensations of an almost meditative rapture. Neil Armstrong, first man on the moon, recalls:

> I remember on the trip home on Apollo 11 it suddenly struck me that that tiny pea, pretty and blue, was the earth. I put up my thumb and shut my eye, and my thumb blotted out the planet earth. I didn't feel like a giant. I felt very, very small.

"You don't look down at the world as an American," three spaceflight veteran Tom Stafford reflected, "but as a human being." Observed Apollo 14's Ed Mitchell:

> Something happens to you out there. . . You develop an instant global consciousness, a people orientation, an intense dissatisfaction with the state of the world and a compulsion to do something about it.

Several spacemen who have admitted sharing in the mysterious soul-stirring that Mitchell describes, have in fact begun to "do something about" the state of their newly-conceived world. Apollo 9's Rusty Schweickart, for instance, entered the field of drug rehabilitation and youth counseling following completion of his tour of duty with the space program. Having returned from an earth-orbital space-walk, it was Schweickart who remarked: "I completely lost my identity as an American astronaut. I felt a part of everyone and everything sweeping past me below."

Other space voyagers have found their extra-terrestrial missions igniting within them a deeper urgency about the relationship of man-to-man and man-to-God. So affected was Apollo 15's Jim Irwin by what he described as the felt "Presence of God" during his lunar odyssey that he gave up his aerospace career altogether to enter the active Christian lay ministry.

What happened to these men in space? Rigorous post-flight "debriefing" and ultra-thorough medical and psychological testing proved that space-journeying had in no way altered them physically. Yet in spirit some had become virtually "new men."

Investigation quickly reveals that their experience does not fit comfortably in any of the rigidly positivist categories of aerospace science. In the cryptic jargon of "mission control" it simply "does not compute" on any empirical scale.

But if the strict tribunal of engineering science permits an appeal to a higher court of human wisdom—one with jurisdiction over man's legitimate experience of the *transcendent* and the spiritual maturation that may come as a result—then something of an analytical verdict is possible.

Indications are that these astronauts underwent a *conversion* in the classical spiritual sense. That is, not so much an instantaneous (and somewhat artificial-sounding) abandonment of decadence for an embracing of piety; but rather an awakening of the heart to an important, previously undiscovered dimension to one's life that unifies all other dimensions into a purposeful, comprehensible whole. Some of history's most influential figures have emerged after the kind of mind-expanding, soul-fusing experience that today's hard-rock balladeer might characterize as "getting it all together!"

The obscure Saul of Tarsus, for example, arose stumbling from his blinding encounter with the Lord on the road to Damascus to become the prototype missionary of Christ. The worldly young Augustine of North Africa, brilliant but restless and undirected, traced the mobilization of his talents for God's service from a mystical moment of reflection on an inspiring passage from St. Paul.

The catalyst for the astronauts' experience of the profound seems to have been the massively enlarged perspective on their "mother Earth" that they gained from space. As eyewitnesses to earth-rise over the moon's gray horizon and to the cloud-veiled world in full circumference, they found themselves exclusively party to a remarkable sight. On a field no more diffuse than a single mind impression, no broader than one camera frame, with imprinted everything that was life-sustaining; all that for them was *home*.

The astronauts saw their world from beyond the close range of physical and metaphysical proximity. The warts, age-lines, and wrinkles—all the great and small imperfections of nature and life as we know it—dissolved from view in the panorama of space. Those who focused back on this planet from the reaches of space perceived their native Earth as a smoothly symmetrical, esthetically pleasing *whole*, refreshingly free of political boundaries, ethnic or racial barriers, and most of all, the scars of human misuse. Inspired by this physical vision of a world at one, they came back determined to translate their aroused "global consciousness" into moral reality as well.

A new age in discovery and exploration began with manned spaceflight. The astronauts, pioneers in the untamed environment of space, expected to meet scientific challenges never faced by men before. But the spiritual chain of events triggered by their observation of the Earth was beyond anticipation. What they *saw* as a round, tranquil body—a floating sign of beauty and harmony in the heavens—they *knew* from experience to be a world disfigured by strife and crying for unity. As far distant in space as these astronauts were from their home planet, in spirit several felt an intensity of affection and concern for all the world and its inhabitants that they had never before known as mere "earth-lubbers."

Some might dismiss these reactions as superficially emotional; the result of an exaggerated homesickness for what the astronauts became increasingly accustomed to referring to as "the good earth."

Certainly it is not uncommon to hold abrupt changes in attitude or behavior suspect. The experience of spiritual uplift some might see as authentic conversion or "interior renewal," others might disbelieve altogether or criticize as religious fanaticism. Sacred Scripture, for instance, records the initial scepticism of the disciple Ananias when told by the Lord in a vision that the notorious Christian-hater Saul had suddenly embraced the faith and was in need of Ananias' ministry (Ac 9:10-19). Earlier in that same book we read of those who "remarked with a sneer" (Ac 2:13) at the Pentecost "conversion" which changed the Apostles from terrified fugitives to crowd-rallying street-preachers. From the cynics' point of view this alleged spiritual awakening sprang less from the overshadowing of the Holy Spirit than the effects of "too much new wine."

However we choose to judge the spaceflight experience Ed Mitchell described as "global consciousness," it is worth noting that Pope Paul VI has spoken in strikingly similar terms when discoursing on the nature of contemporary religious experience for modern man, and on the role of the Church in his life:

> Sharing the noble aspirations of men and suffering when she sees them not satisfied, (The Church) wishes to help them attain their full flowering, and that is why she offers men what she possesses as her characteristic attribute: a global vision of man and of the human race.[1]

Moreover as a keynote theme of the Second Vatican Council's *Constitution on The Church in The Modern World*, the Fathers of that Council encourage today's Christian to formulate his sense of values and responsibilities *in* the world from at least an imaginary space-traveler's vantage point overlooking the *whole* of it:

> Every day human interdependence grows more tightly drawn and spreads by degrees over the whole world.

---

1. *On The Development of Peoples*, Part II, #13.

As a result . . . every social group must take account
of the legitimate needs and aspirations of other groups,
and even of the general welfare of the entire human
family.[2]

Galileo's astronomy, the modern evolutionary theory of
Darwin, and the behaviorist revolution sparked by Freud
have successfully spoiled detente between the cultural super-
powers Science and Religion. In light of a relationship between the two often suspicious at best, bitterly hostile at
worst, hasty or extravagant conclusions ought to be avoided
when investigating the "conversion" experience of the astronauts. Nevertheless, in mining the common lode of contemporary man's motivating drives and unrequited needs, a
Church in process of renewal and a scientific project of un-
precedented magnitude and implications for man's future
have apparently both struck the same rich vein: a universal
craving for a healing reconciliation of man with his fellow
human beings, with nature, and with God.

Ironically, in our age of supersonic travel and globe-
shrinking instantaneous communications, we find ourselves
more antagonized than ever by the gremlins of alienation
and estrangement. On a purely sociological level "progress"
and "efficiency" have masked themselves too often as dis-
appointing euphemisms for assembly-line procedures that
isolate individuals and smother initiative, talent, and creativ-
ity. The astronauts whom we quote above provide some wise
commentary on the agony as well as the ecstasy of technological achievement. Like wingmen skating on the very circumference of an ice rink whip-crack game, they were cata-
pulted into orbit through the impetus of massive human energies painstakingly mobilized and interlocked exclusively for
that purpose. Once propelled into space, the technological

2. Chapter II, paragraph #26.

magnitude of their successful "great leap for all mankind" supplied stark contrast to the few, meager steps they recalled men were taking toward peace, justice, freedom, prosperity and dignity for all on the slowly revolving earth below.

Current events give us even more graphic evidence of modern man unreconciled and suffering deeply from his divisions. With the "highest standard of living in the world" the United States—for all its material advantages—exemplifies as well as any society the characteristics of dehumanizing, demoralizing fragmentation. In just a little over a decade our nation has been pummelled by waves of racial violence, generational conflict, searing political strife, extraordinary governmental corruption and public trust betrayal, and the soul-rending excruciation of the Southeast Asia war.

In clinical terms such disintegration at the organismic stage of social development suggests serious dysfunction at the "cellular"—the personal—stage. To us this means simply that the health and quality of our personal lives—even in an age of flesh-healing antibiotic "wonder drugs"—remains subject to attack by a wide assortment of afflictions of the spirit. In addition to the more overt species of personality breakdown we attribute to the presence of neurotic or even psychotic symptoms in those among us who are most obviously distressed, experts are quick to point out that the complexity and uncertainties of modern life take their toll on us all. Who of us, for instance, is immune from the effects of what Teilhard de Chardin described as "rapidation": the "future-shocked" compression of chaotic past and ambiguous future into an anxiety-ridden present?

To what shall I compare this generation? We seem in many ways like those milling masses of the uncertain and unfulfilled whom Jesus sighed over, preached to, prayed for, and even fed. Long on messianic expectations while short on personal zeal, boastful yet insecure, conscious of price but ignorant of value, technologically sophisticated yet culturally immature; our meanderings in search of spiritual authenticity mark so many of us as latter-day "reeds shaking in the wind"—post-agrarian "sheep without a shepherd."

"But what did you come out to see?" The thousands who flocked to Jesus came not to hear scholar-like philosophizing on *why* they were poor, sick, or troubled, but to receive from him a plain-spoken alternative to life as they knew it. In a word Jesus offered *salvation*. In point of fact he eschewed the vague, pie-in-the-sky sanctimony we customarily associate with that word, for speech about it bristling with "authority" and substantiating actions loaded with power. By calling out the demons that tormented, frightened, and divided real persons living along the shores of Galilee during the age of Augustus Caesar, he meant to assure men of every subsequent era that no dark "principalities and powers"— whatever their particular historical shape—could hold sway where his name was invoked and his Kingdom welcomed.

What must we do to be saved? Repent! Change! "Now is the acceptable time!" St. Mark who sees Jesus primarily as a man of action, quotes these exclamations as the very first words of the Master at the outset of his public life. John the Baptist and the Old Testament prophets before him had preached to Israel in much the same terms. But while John's was a "baptism of repentance"—a summons to the individual to live more uprightly lest he incur God's wrath, the baptism of Jesus inaugurated *reconciliation* between God and man through the healing power of divine love. "I baptize with water," said John, "*he* will baptize with the Holy Spirit and fire!" John recognized that his ministry was limited to a call for man's moral reformation. In Jesus John rightly discerned the unlimited capacity to effect man's *transformation* in God.

The visible sign of such transformation's beginnings— the seal of genuine *conversion in Christ*—is the presence of a growing *unity*. Having encountered Jesus ever so briefly, yet somehow touched by the Spirit enlivening him, the dozen who would become his Apostles each found it impossible to resume the niche in life he had been filling before coming face to face with this mysterious stranger. Putting aside nets and ledgers they came together forming the first community of his followers. Where John the Baptist (not to mention the age-old strain of fundamentalist revivalism) could appeal only to one's private, subjective understanding and acceptance of reform, *ecclesia* (lit. "gathering together") developed spontaneously among those who identified themselves as brothers and sisters in the Lord Jesus—the only-begotten Son of their common Father. The Acts of the Apostles describes in some detail the nature of the primitive Church as the communion of those who—baptized in Christ—strove through common prayer, sharing of material possessions, and "the breaking of the bread," to live the reconciled life in God they had received in the Risen Lord.

Looking back over the nearly two millennia of its history, the Church sees several major developments in Western civilization brought on by the collective urge to make the kind of transformative *new beginning* called for in the Gospel as a constitutive part of the Kingdom's coming. At one era compulsion to respond to God in a communitarian and devotional way led masses of the faithful on religious pilgrimage. At another, the drive to express Christian spirituality in a creative as well as mass-cultural way blossomed through the medium of architecture. By the later Middle Ages virtually every population center of European Christendom could boast of ornate churches and cathedrals erected over the course of several generations through the common, unflagging—often lifetime—efforts of the most gifted artisans and the lowliest laborers. The flowering of monasticism may have represented the noblest—the Crusades probably the most adulterated—of the fervid outpourings of medieval Christian man's longing to fashion a community of persons and pursuits in the Gospel tradition.

What then do terms such as "conversion," "salvation," "transformation," and "repentance" mean in the "now" of the space age? If cathedral-building and pilgrimaging once signified the upward and outward striving of the faithful in community toward their God, the charism Pope Paul identifies as "global vision" in the modern Church suggests that ours is a particularly "acceptable time" for growth in that unifying spiritual process St. Paul described as advancement "from faith to faith."

There is ample evidence that the Holy Spirit is guiding the post-conciliar Church toward the kind of consciousness-expansion that overtook the astronauts as they viewed the soft, blue, whole Earth from their vantage point in space. This new spiritual *Weltanschauung* is evident, for instance, in Vatican II's affirmation of religious liberty and the Council's teachings on the respect owed moral and doctrinal decisions of the informed personal conscience. It is highly visible in the progress of the ecumenical movement over the past decade. Important dialogue has been carried on and conciliatory overtures made between the separated Christian communions, between Christian and Jew, between Christian and Marxist atheist, between Christianity and the Eastern religions. Pictures of Roman Pontiff embracing Anglican Archbishop and Orthodox Patriarch have given millions hopeful encouragement that the term "separated brethren" may at last be heading for obsolescence. The stepped-up involvement of the Catholic Church in promoting interracial harmony, international understanding, and gap-closing between rich and poor classes; developed and underdeveloped nations; powerful and powerless peoples; the steady supplanting of polemics that divide with gestures that can help unite; *all of these* mark a renewed awakening to the power of Christ's Lordship in the world.

As welcome and promising as these developments have been, commentators on the religious scene today remind us more and more emphatically that structural reform and growing institutional openness can only be useful to the advancement of God's Kingdom when complemented by the interior spiritual renewal—conversion—of the individual. In proclaiming the 1974-75 Holy Year of Reconciliation Pope Paul VI called for just this kind of personal reinvigoration. Importantly, in his allocution outlining the Holy Year's theme, the Holy Father recognized the need not only for a resurgence of moral idealism in everyday life, but a reconstructive healing of those alienation wounds afflicting persons in every segment of modern society:

> The essential concept of the Holy Year . . . is the interior renewal of man: of the thoughtful man, who in his thinking has lost the certainty of truth; of the working man, who in his work has realized that he is so extroverted that he no longer is sufficiently in touch with his inner self; of the man enjoying life who so amuses himself and has so many exciting ways to gain pleasurable experience that he soon feels bored and disillusioned. . . Man must be renewed from within. This is what the Gospel calls conversion, penance, and change of heart. It is the process of self-rebirth. . .**

These words of Pope Paul reaffirm a simple but crucial truth of our faith. To be "converted," in the fullest, most genuine sense of the term, means an entering-into life at the point of Christ. To be where He is, envision what He sees, imitate what He does—in sum, to live as He lives—is to be

---

** Announcement of 1975 Holy Year, May 9, 1973.

fully alive and at one with "the length and breadth, height and depth" of His Creation. Further, the action of conversion is, as the Holy Father says, a *process*. As such it involves time, struggle, prayer, discernment, cooperation, understanding— all the dynamics that constitute *virtuous change*. "Process" means a movement toward full flowering that begins with a seminal "dying." It includes a letting-go as well as a picking- up. It is an invitation to conceive one's life always within the stage of "greenwood"—supple to the Breath of the Holy Spirit and flexible so as to weather the stresses and challenges of life while remaining firmly rooted.

In many ways we are just now emerging as a Church from the grip of the Middle Ages. Scholastic philosophy which so powerfully influenced the direction of theology in the Western Church for many centuries dealt principally in the timeless and immutable. The Second Vatican Council's approval of the "Pilgrim Church" model recognized contemporary man's justifiable concern with life-in-motion. Freedom, growth, response, renewal—these are as integral to the Revealed Truth of Scripture as are "one, holy, catholic and apostolic." Hence the "simplicity" of our faith requires our participation in it as well as our belief in it. Folksinger Judy Collins' rendition of the old Quaker hymn "Simple Gifts" explains this well:

> Tis the gift to be simple, tis the gift to be free;
> Tis the gift to come down where we ought to be.
> And when we are in the place just right,
> We'll be in the valley of Love and Delight.
> When true Simplicity is gained,
> To bow and to bend we will not be ashamed;
> To turn, to turn, t'will be our delight,
> Till by turning, turning, we come round right.**

** Copyright Elektra Records. Album *Whales* & *Nightingales*.

The following chapters are written in the belief that the process of rebirth in Christ—the process of reconciliation—deserves the particular attention the Church is calling to it at this moment in history. Since the Gospels treat the mission of Christ largely in terms of freeing man for the "life-more-abundantly" that is received through communion with neighbor and union with the Father through love, that responsibility is ours as heirs and propagators of the Apostolic community of faith. Yet our efforts to see Christ active and to cooperate with His Spirit in the labor of rebirth and re-creation tend to be hampered by a few chronic religious ailments that seem widespread among our Catholic congregations today, and which rate our attention in the pages ahead.

Briefly, while more traditionalist voices decry what they interpret as "confusion" in the post-Vatican II Church, this author senses that contemporary Catholics are faced with problems or doubts in their practice of faith more accurately ascribed to *diffusion;* that is, irregular, arrested, or imbalanced development in areas where growth toward religious maturity demands steady, well-integrated progress. In terms of our *conversion process* we lack for the most part a *unifying experience* of what Scripture says, what the Church teaches, what the Sacraments celebrate, and what we are truly responsible for in our Christian moral lives.

For example, many churchgoers ostensibly hungering and thirsting for the nourishing bread of the Scriptures have long been forced to settle for a steady diet of stones. In the Catholic community symptoms of spiritual malnutrition are often traceable to educational backgrounds in the faith lacking in the fundamentals of Old and New Testament understanding. Most adults sitting in our pews today have been schooled in their faith through the tractate approach of the Baltimore catechism. While heavily weighted toward systematic arrangement of commandments, precepts, virtues, etc. and indebted to precise doctrinal formulation "packaging" for the transmission of religious truths, the Scriptures— under this educational schema—were comparatively lightly culled. More often than not, when Scripture was considered it was approached less as an original font of revealed truth than as an apologetic "backup" useful mainly for substantiating whatever moral or dogmatic principle was being offered.

Efforts at renewal have taught us how theological idioms or religious terminology can—through overworked usage— take on a life of their own to the detriment of the truths they once helped to relate. "Soldier of Christ," for example, was once the standard popular descriptive for what one became at Confirmation. Presently though, as renewed catechesis has expanded our appreciation of Confirmation as a "sacrament of initiation" into the manifold responsibilities and privileges of Christian community membership, the notion of "soldier of Christ" can easily stand replacement by terms that acknowledge the wide-ranging talents and charisms of the Holy Spirit that the sacrament bears to each candidate for the upbuilding of all. Further, in our war-sensitized time and culture, the term "soldier" connotes something more militarist then militant, and its use in a sacred setting must be questioned in an age when the reigning Pontiff cries out before the United Nations General Assembly "No more war!"

Misunderstanding or misinterpretation of religious phraseology compounds our diffusion dilemma. Our manuals, for instance, describe the action of Christ in transmitting His Spirit to the ages as "instituting" the sacraments. This perfectly legitimate and orthodox term "institute" is familiar to every catechized Catholic. Indications are, however, that as *institute* interchanges all too easily in the popular mind with *install*, an unsatisfactorily static idea of sacramentality has developed among many; one which tends to remove the saving action of the Lord Jesus from its rightful immediacy in the sacrament, placing it back somewhere in distant space and ancient time. Thus as a practical working explanation of some Catholics' adherence to Church discipline regarding attendance at Sunday Mass, reception of Communion, confessing of sins, etc., is an unhappy concept which in fact relegates Christ to the status of a holy *plumber*. The overall divine plan—as perceived through this limited "institution" model—has Jesus first and foremost concerned with installing the necessary "fixtures" (the Sacraments) through which the properly-regulated flow of divine graces might continue to be channelled to man following Jesus' departure from the scene. A strong argument can be made, based on this peculiar Christology, for a strict observance of obligations pertaining to attendance at the Sacraments. But the fidelity of the New Testament to the central act of Jesus Christ—proclaiming the new, decisive era in history that is the Reign of God—may well be sacrificed in the process. Invariably, through catechesis out of touch with the central themes of Scripture, the Sacraments become denuded of their appeal and their authenticity as sign-celebrations re-presenting God's ongoing Saving action, and assume instead the characteristic of drably functional spigots from which, from time to time, the faithful are obliged to drink. With the distortion of doctrine comes the misconstruction of Sacrament, abuse of liturgy, and muddling of the Christian's extraordinary moral responsibilities as a follower of the living, Redeeming Christ.

For many of us, then, who seek to be well-informed, actively-participating members of our Catholic Church, a more well-rounded understanding of Scriptural message, Church teaching, sacrament celebration, and practical life style as *integrated parts* of the whole Christian existence ranks high on the scale of our priorities for "reconciliation."

We make no pretensions to accomplish all that within the limitations of this book. As an example of such integration, however, we do hope to develop something of a Scriptural-Sacramental-practical approach to the issue of man's estrangement, leading into some thoughts on the nature today of that traditional source of Catholic spiritual rebirth—the Sacrament of Penance.

In every age of the Church Penance has adapted itself to the particular needs of the faithful, enabling them to experience God's unfailing forgiveness. In a much earlier age when the *ordo penitentiae* was filled with sinners excluded from the body of worshipping believers it was a clearcut matter to see what the sinner lacked and what he sought in terms of reconciliation. Such is not the case today. Impersonal "service station" routinizing of the sacrament has left many unclear as to what Penance really has to offer them, what they are really estranged from, and what they really can do to feel more fully united to the Body of Christ in which they claim membership. It seems safe to say that one major reason for the heavy "attrition rate" evident in the number of confession-goers today is a simple lack of consciousness on the part of non-penitents that they are in any way *apart* from anything.

Real conversion begins only when one begins to sense that "something is missing"—something essential for growth toward "life to the full" that Jesus promised and proclaimed. Among other major theologians of our time, Edward Schillebeeckx suggests that what weakens the potential of religion to illumine and integrate man's life today amounts not so much to a crisis of *belief*—orthodoxy—as it does to one of *orthopraxis*: an absence of a motivating vision of God's Kingdom being advanced, and hence a moral inertia when it comes to conceiving ourselves as participants in the Saving Action of Christ as it proceeds right now. We confess, for example, but do we truly "convert"? We lead socially "respectable" lives—but shouldn't they be grace-conscious heroic ones? We are God-fearing, yet often far from God-loving. Ironically, having listened passively to innumerable Sunday sermons, we remain largely unevangelized—touched rarely if ever by a deep-felt personal awareness that the Lord is doing for us through His Spirit what he did of old when he appeared in the flesh. The active, the *doing* Word of God that heals wounds and gives sight—the Word that calls us to wholeness of self and unity in the love of our Father—seems to be heard much less frequently than it is uttered.

However self-critical we wish to be in regard to the barricades and defenses we can raise to shut ourselves off from God's Word, we have a solid basis for hope in the knowledge that it is precisely to people like ourselves that God's Saving Word has been spoken. The more resistant we see ourselves to that Word, the more we can identify with the "hardness of heart" understood as the real essence of sin in both Old and New Testament Scripture. The more too can we appreciate the praises offered God in those Scriptures by those who have experienced liberation from that spiritual affliction.

In the pages that follow, our aim will be to put ourselves in the archetypal roles Scripture assigns alienated man. Let us see how the Lord will act out the mystery of our re-creation as we present ourselves to him in the form described by the Psalmist—"a people yet unborn."

Chapter II

Creation and Re-Creation:
Moral Understanding in the Old Testament

Scholars tell us that most cultures of the ancient Near East developed myths to account for the beginnings of creation. Though the plots and characters varied in the myths of differing peoples the basic story lines were often similar. Virtually all these tales explained that things came to be only after a divisive clash or reproductive mating of two or more godlike forces. For instance, in the *Enuma Elish*, the Babylonian epic dating back at least 3000 years, all begins with the coupling of the primordial male and female deities Apsu and Tiamat. From their union is born the all-powerful Marduk who ultimately does battle with Tiamat, slays her, and constructs the cosmos from the material of her carcass. Other civilizations developed their myths of creation around the wars and intrigues of good and evil spirits; the forces of darkness versus those of light. Dualism was a common feature of ancient thinking. Nothing new could materialize without an action-reaction process.

The Old Testament account of creation in Genesis breaks sharply with the pagan dualist schema. The tenet unique to the cosmology of primitive Israel taught that in the beginning there was but One. Israel's faith flowed from the belief that Yahweh—the One Perfect and sufficient unto Himself—freely fashioned all creation, blessing it with a harmony, an integrity, a wholeness of being that reflected an image and likeness of Himself:

> The heavens declare the glory of God,
> and the firmament proclaims his handiwork! (Ps 19)

The age-old formula of Israel's faith is chanted in the Hebrew prayer invitatory: "Hear oh Israel, the Lord Our God, the Lord is One!" Yet we know—and the compilers of Genesis knew—that not all in creation mirrors God's at-one-ment. Sin, suffering, and death are abroad in nature. Man is troubled by inner conflict and ravaged by social divisions. But because no anti-God, no co-equal Force of Darkness or host of malevolent spirits were even thinkable in the early religious mentality of Israel, how were such flaws in the divine plan to be explained?

The answer of Genesis, of course, is that evil is not of God's doing. Man, the noblest of creatures (and the only one with sufficient power and freedom to promote major disorder) is branded the villain. As the cartoon character Pogo would have it, "we have met the enemy, and he is *us!*"

The simple tale of a man, a woman, a fruit tree and a snake has been taught to us as a story of disobedience punished. Yet much more is revealed in the subtler details of the Fall account that pertain directly to our efforts at self-understanding and moral development today.

In modern physics the famed Second Law of Thermodynamics holds that all matter left untended by related natural forces (gravitation, atomic reaction, electro-magnetism, etc.) will tend toward its most extreme state of dissolution. Less elegantly stated, things unheld together will fly apart. Analogously, the story of the Fall in Genesis analyzes the condition of man, of society—indeed, all of nature—as suffering the effects of man's prideful attempt to alter the fundamental relationship established with him by God. Having failed to stand *above* God man is left *apart* from Him. Further, man's rebellious unwillingness to accept a natural harmonious relationship with God sends shock waves of damaging distortion through all other relationships obtaining in creation.

Succumbing to the temptation of the forbidden fruit, Adam and Eve find that having stepped apart from God they have stepped apart from each other:

> The woman saw that the tree was good for food, pleasing to the eyes, and desirable for gaining wisdom. So she took some of its fruit and ate it; and she also gave some to her husband, who was with her, and he ate it. Then the eyes of both of them were opened, and they realized that they were naked; so they sewed fig leaves together and made loincloths for themselves.
>
> (Gn 3: 6-8)

The wisdom of Genesis finds man's state of sudden self-consciousness prima facie evidence of his sin. Shame is the sensation of feeling inadequate while being spotlighted. The story uses the image of shame at first perception of physical nakedness to illustrate the unsatisfactory self-image Adam and Eve discover as their "eyes open" to the new situation of life-after-sin. No longer "one" but two, sin has produced in them an isolating fission.

While they hasten to cover those physical parts that most graphically distinguish them, they cannot escape being bared to each other and to themselves in their *weakness* (having failed to supersede God), their *loneliness* (having excluded themselves from the shelter of God's care), and their *vulnerability* to the punitive effects of their own sin. Moreover they are shamed by their exposure to each other as betrayers of God and thus potential betrayers of one another. Understandably their moral act of flight from God is duplicated in their troubled rush from His summoning call. Where love and confidence would once have hastened Adam and Eve to God's side for a walk together "in the cool of the evening," now fearful guile and insecurity drive them to hide from His voice.

The sinful results of the Fall spread quickly. The expulsion of Adam and Eve from the Garden of Eden symbolizes man's loss of dominion over the forces of nature and signals a new subjection to their ravages. Even the animal kingdom suffers a divorce from peaceful communion with man as the snake is cursed by God. Like waves radiating from a pebble tossed into a becalmed pool, sin rapidly gains social extension. Genesis records the fratricide of Cain and the cancerous corruption of the whole human community. Finally, with the moral stage set for a Wagnerian denouement, the wrath of God explodes upon a world re-plunged into chaos by sin and the purgative waters of the Great Flood close upon the earth.

The teaching Church recognizes that the inspired writings of the Creation and Fall accounts are not designed to provide an historically precise nor scientifically factual record. As literary vehicles their aim is to transmit the moral truth of man's timeless need for self-transcendence and a reconstructive healing of the mysterious rifts that plague his nature. More than 1000 years after the first campfire sharing of these Semitic tales, St. Paul would identify himself as a son of Adam and an heir to his legacy of alienation:

> I cannot even understand my own actions. I do not do what I want to do but what I hate. . . I know that no good dwells in me, that is, in my flesh; the desire to do right is there, but not the power. What happens is that I do, not the good I will to do, but the evil I do not intend. . . My inner self agrees with the law of God, but I see in my body's members another law at war

with the law of my mind. . . What a wretched man am I! (Rm 7: 15 ff)

Offering the first Testamental statement on a cosmos "groaning in travail," Genesis admits of evil, absurdity, and tragedy entering upon the world's stage impairing man's power to discern truth and live uprightly. The Fall has left man with a distorted, fragmented view of reality. He "sees" only as through a glass darkly.

There is, of course, an ageless fascination about man's struggle with his own dehumanizing tendencies. The moral ambiguity and restlessness of the human spirit have been pondered in treatises from Heraclitus to Heidegger, and celebrated in the arts from Sophocles to Picasso. Modern Jewish philosopher Martin Buber, writing from a distinctively Biblical orientation, relates some of the key insights of Genesis to what the leading existentialist thinkers of our era have labeled man's "crisis in intersubjectivity."

Buber speaks of the fundamental human difficulties resulting from man's limited ability to establish relationships with all outside himself. To identify an other as "thou," Buber says, is to acknowledge both the presence of inherent value in that other, and the existence of a bond of relationship linking oneself to the *thou*. Buber points out, however, that in most real cases we tend to identify an other not as an esteemed *thou*, but merely as a functional "it." As a result, rather than devoting energy to the cultivating and refining of relationships, we tend to do just the opposite: isolating ourselves against whatever is "foreign" or outside ourselves. When not withdrawing in fear from *its* we conceive as threatening, or ignoring those we predetermine as unuseful, we most often snatch condescendingly at those others we regard as "tools"—subservient to our needs and subject to our exploitation.

Buber's analysis coincides with what Genesis reveals as the real nature of sin; that is, a *condition of separation*—a *being-apart* from an authentic relationship with God and His Creation.

Unhappily, in an overeagerness to simplify, Christian moral education has sometimes mistakenly conveyed the idea that "sin" strictly means discontinuous acts of commission or omission, distinguishable only in mortal or venial degree. To the contrary, the Fall account teaches that at its ground sin is a *situation;* the life-smothering inward-turning upon oneself that Kierkegaard called "the sickness unto death." Having opted for self-centeredness in the Garden, man is now cursed by it in the world.

THE "NEW HEART"—THE BEGINNINGS OF RESTORATION

Though innocence is lost in the Garden of Eden, hope is born. Even as Adam and Eve are exiled from Paradise the Word of God rebukes the serpent for his mischief and prophesies the containment of his death-leading powers of temptation (Gn 3:14-15). Thus Genesis provides early reassurance that despite his misery fallen man need not despair. In the present state of man's tragedy Scripture perceives raw material for God's glory through a great future act of redeeming reconciliation.

Genesis also supplies an uplifting climax to the devastation of the Deluge. The survival of Noah and his family marks the introduction of the *remnant theme*—a classic Old Testament pattern in which those relatively few who remain faithful to God in spite of adversity live to enjoy His favor, while greater numbers of the sinful and faithless perish. The "bow in the clouds" (Gn 9:1-7) seals the first of the major Scriptural *covenants* as God forswears total annihilation as a means of punishment, pledging never to abandon man or creation.

Covenant is an important concept in the faith of Israel. In virtually every theophany recorded in the Old Testament some reference is made to God's unflinching fidelity to His Chosen People, and to their responsibilities in return for His care. "I will be your God and you shall be my people!" (Jr 7:23; Ezk 11:20). Under the terms of their divine compact Israel understood God's intention to reopen a channel of communication with man through a nation uniquely His own; a channel through which His Word, Law, and blessing could flow freely once again.

The presence of Covenant at the center of Israel's religious experience taught her (sometimes painfully) of God's "jealousy" on her behalf. The Chosen People learned that while theirs was a Lord "slow to anger and abounding in kindness" (Ps 86), He was most adamant in demanding their absolute trust. While patient with Israel's frequent religious obstinacies, and liberal in pardoning transgressions of His rule, the Lord God shows Himself utterly intolerant of idolatry. He will have no other gods before Him—be they artifact idols or supercilious creatures.

"Put not your trust in princes; in man in whom there is no salvation!" (Ps 146). In contrast to the humanist idealism characteristic of ancient Greco-Roman culture (and powerfully instrumental in the subsequent growth of modern Western civilization), the Old Testament early on disavows all rationalist notions of the "indefinite perfectability" of man. The scars of human estrangement and moral instability are plain to see, and Old Testament lore records the swiftness and severity of divine chastisements visited on the proud and self-righteous.

Even such an apparently well-intentioned—if embarrass-

ingly simplistic—scheme to reach God as was devised by the
builders of the Babel Tower ignites the Lord's anger and
earns His curse. Drawing a parallel with the original power-
play of Adam and Eve, the insight of Genesis sees the Tower's erection as an act of sinful presumption; man seduced
once more by the pathetic idea that God can be made acces-
sible (and thus rendered subject to man in some degree) by
man's act of will and application of his resources. In a poetic
act of retribution those who sought self-induced communication with God suddenly find themselves unable to com-
municate even with each other.

The Old Testament sees God patiently maneuvering to
gain man's undivided attention to *His* plan for salvation
through something of a "carrot and stick" approach. The
Lord holds out hope to man through the Covenant promises
of ultimate deliverance, while prodding him to acknowledge
that such deliverance can come only through a total giving-
over of himself to God. The road God sets before man, the
road often winding and sometimes fearful, is that of *faith*.

The all-time model traveler of that road is the patriarch
Abraham. Originally identified as "Abram," this simple,
otherwise undistinguished shepherd receives God's call to
act as the first of the great *servant-leader* figures of the Old
Testament. He is asked to abandon all that is familiar to him:
his land, his occupation, even his name; and to follow with
unwavering confidence the God Who will lead him on a
mysterious journey to an unknown destination for reasons
undisclosed. As Genesis details Abram's adventures it becomes clear that his radically new identity and life-style as
Abraham constitutes a type of the *new man* God proposes to
re-create from the spiritually-scarred human remains of
Adam and Eve.

The Scriptural message is clear. For fallen mankind—
embodied in the character of Abram—two conditions are

essential for the process of intimate God-man reunion to begin: a willingness to undergo drastic change from a self-centered pattern of living to an Other-centered one; and a willingness to let God lead the way. The overture for reconciliation the Lord makes toward man in the Old Testament takes primary shape in God's appeal for man's acceptance of a new identity; a new understanding of his own personhood; in the Semitic idiom—to accept a new "heart."

Man's heart in the primitive Old Testament mentality was the focal point of his existence. Man's most important bodily organ, the heart was thought to be the sustaining center of all life's biological and psychological functions. The heart represented the seat of all intellectual, spiritual, and moral activity in the ancient Jewish physiology. The cry of the Psalmist in later Testamental literature

> A clean heart create for me O God,
> And a steadfast spirit renew within me! (Ps 51:10)

discloses Israel's understanding that relations between God and man must be established at the highest level of human capacity—that of moral judgment and decision-making as it occurred within man's "heart."

Such an acknowledgement of God-man relationship and communication centering upon man's *moral behavior* is a crucial one in Revelation. For it signifies Israel's departure from the religious viewpoint of virtually the entire "pagan" world.

THE LAW IN ANCIENT ISRAEL: PERSONAL CALL AND COMMUNAL RESPONSE TO MORALITY

To appreciate the full significance of the considerations that follow, a careful reminder is in order: no inherent relationship exists between religion and morality.

In fact, as a general anthropological rule, primitive man's sense of the sacred focused on nature—not behavior—

as the point of contact with the divine. The movements of sun, moon, and stars; the phenomena of rain, snow, lightning, clouds, fire and water; the mysteries of birth, growth, life, death, and change in nature—all primitive man's experiences of forces around him otherwise beyond his power to understand—he tended to attribute to the supernatural workings of an unseen world of spirits or gods.

The growth within almost all early civilizations of some religious cult that included witch doctors or shamans, symbolic dress and actions, often elaborate ceremonial rites, indicates the importance these societies attached to gaining favor with the deities of nature. In all of this, one's personal or social *ethical* conduct often held little if any religious significance. For these gods were thought of as purely *impersonal* deities; strong forces influential in determining man's fortune or destiny, yet largely uninvolved in man's moral judgments. Thus, no arbitrary codes of law or behavior (outside cultic practice) were associated with them.

Contrasting with the pagan notion of impersonal deity, Israel's experience was of a Personal God deeply interested and active in human affairs. Israel saw her God as the One Lord of *history* Whose workings were perceptible not in the whims of fortune or vagaries of nature, but in the life of that small society which knew itself to be His Chosen People. In essence, the Old Testament is Israel's interpretation of her own history; an interpretation which links personal conduct and social behavior to unique encounters with the Living God.

Moreover, as the Covenant theme dramatizes in God's dealings with Noah, Abraham, and Moses, the Lord of History does not seek appeasement or flattery by ritual cultic practices. Israel's God challenges His People to *follow Him* to a new, Promised Land, to a new freedom, and to a new identity as a nation.

What sort of response, then, does this God of Israel seek if not in ceremonial cult? The God Who speaks to the *heart* of man—to the most profound aspect of his being—expects a response from that same heart. It is from man's *person*-ality, from his attitude and character, from his regard for himself and others that God wants to hear. Unless a man's heart speaks with the voice of moral uprightness, his prayers and cultic offerings are not only futile, they are an abomination:

> What care I for the number of your sacrifices? says the Lord. I have had enough of whole-burnt rams and fat of fatlings;
> In the blood of calves, lambs, and goats I find no pleasure. Your new moons and festivals I detest; they weigh me down, I tire of the load.
> When you spread out your hands I close my eyes to you; though you pray the more I will not listen.
> Your hands are full of blood! Wash yourselves clean! Put away your misdeed from before my eyes; cease doing evil; learn to do good.
> Make justice your aim; redress the wronged, hear the orphan's plea, defend the widow. Come now, let us set things right, says the Lord. (Is 1:11 ff)

Such oracles of God's displeasure with man's sinfulness are characteristic of the Prophetic literature. Yet, as the Isaiah passage suggests, the Old Testament never permits the threat of chastisement nor the pervasiveness of sin to overshadow the fundamental proclamation of promise and hope.

God's glory will not be thwarted by waywardness or rebellion, nor will it accept satisfaction in the faithfulness of just a few. Before the eyes of Abraham, the first of His Patriarchs, the Lord unfurls the majestic vision that He will set before each succeeding leader of His People. It portrays a once-fallen mankind ultimately resurgent in love and fidelity, stretching out before the Saving Lord in numbers ". . . as

countless as the stars of the sky and the sands of the seashore"
(Gn 22:17). To our superabundant joy as believers, there
is as much grandeur about God's design for man's redemption chronicled in later Old Testament writing as Genesis
provides in the account of man's advent in creation:

> I will take you away from among the nations, gather
> you from all the foreign lands, and bring you back to
> your own land . . . I will give you a new heart and
> place a new spirit within you, taking from your bodies
> your stony hearts and giving you natural hearts . . .
> 'This desolate land has been made into a Garden of
> Eden,' [the nations] shall say. Thus [they] shall know
> that I, the Lord, have rebuilt what was destroyed and
> replanted what was desolate. I, the Lord, have prom-
> ised, and I will do it! (Ezk 36:24ff)

The Eden of old had been the spawning ground for a
whirlwind of spiritual devastation. God elected not to re-
strain the ravaging tide of destructiveness loosed by sin, but
rather to follow in its havoc-strewn path salvaging the wreck-
age that evil was making of His world. The patient Lord of
Israel, then, reveals Himself as much a *pursuer* of his storm-
shocked people as He is their chieftain. As rich in tenderness
as He is strong in might, the Lord trails in the wake of the
primal tornado comforting, healing and promising to restore
to wholeness what the furies of evil have sought to blast
away.

Since we are especially interested in what the Scriptures
tell us of reconciliation, God's pattern of retracing after
despoiled creation is an important one to follow. First, because the storm of evil first touched down upon individuals
(Adam and Eve), the graces of reconciliation make their
initial appearance in the singular "new man" model of Abraham. Scriptural attention then turns to the divine strategy
for combatting the epidemic effect of evil in society.

If sin's disintegrating force in society is represented in

the debacle of Babel, the ideal of God-centered community cohesiveness makes its appearance in the *Law* handed down from God through Moses. Embellished as it is with detailed descriptions of proper social, familial, sexual, dietary, hygienic, and cultural conduct, the Law as it is given on Mount Sinai marks a new era in the relationship of God and man.

In the view of the prophet Jeremiah, obedience to the Law fulfills the individual Israelite as a person, links him in the most decisive fashion to the Chosen race, and constitutes the sole and definitive way to reconciliation with the Almighty:

> This is the covenant I will make with the house of Israel says the Lord. I will place my law within them and write it on their hearts. . . No longer will they have need to teach their friends and kinsmen how to know the Lord. All, from least to greatest shall know me, says the Lord, for I will forgive their evildoing and remember their sin no more. (Jr 31:33-34)

Unlike national codes such as the United States Constitution, the Mosaic Law unifies rather than separates the concepts of religion and state. Not only does the Law provide a basis in civil statute and uniform social convention for the fashioning of Israel as a political entity, but the attribution of its precepts to God Himself is unique in the primitive world.

In the Old Testament vision the Law supplies a stabilizing effect for man, drawing precisely defined limits within which he may act morally. Thus the anxiety created by the possibility of abusing unrestricted freedom (as described in Genesis) is eased. Fundamentally, the Law in the theology of Israel provides practical applications for the rightly-directed, yet general promptings of man's "new heart." Further, the Law in Israelite understanding constitutes a new meeting ground for God and man. Religious ceremony and devotional practices are understood as celebrations symbolically offering the fruits of acceptable personal and communal conduct to the Lord. Right order, harmony in creation, peace among men—the qualities severely eroded in Adam's fall—resurface as ideals under the aegis of the Law. But, as we shall see, they are ideals to be defined in God's terms, not in man's.

RIGHTEOUSNESS—KEYSTONE OF OLD TESTAMENT ETHICS

Insofar as it unifies the Israelites and elevates consciousness of their responsibilities before God, the Law is an instrument of divine reconciliation. Underlying that Law is the Old Testament concept of Justice (more effectively translated "righteousness"). By and large our sense of appreciation for *Christian* morality suffers from an ignorance of what this important principle *supplied* as well as what it lacked as a conciliatory factor in the God-man relationship. Its consideration is a necessary prelude to the extraordinary teaching of Jesus on the unity of God and man in love.

We note at once that Old Testament Law is really no more inherently enlightened or humanitarian than the codes of behavior extant among other primitive peoples. Though more extensive and minutely detailed than most pagan codes and, of course, distinct by virtue of Israel's belief in its divine origin, the Mosaic Law tends toward scrupulous legalism and even crudity. Hard-line finality, a barbarous sense of equity, and outright mandates for the slaughter of serious offenders are found in ample measure throughout Leviticus and Deuteronomy:

> Anyone who inflicts an injury on his neighbor shall receive the same in return. Limb for limb, eye for eye, tooth for tooth! (Lv 24:19-20)

> This is how you must deal with [the pagan nations]: Tear down their altars, smash their sacred pillars,

> chop down their sacred poles, and destroy their idols by fire. . . You shall consume all the nations which the Lord God will deliver up to you. You are not to look on them with pity. . . You will rout them utterly until they are annihilated. (Dt 7:5, 16, 23)

> When two men are fighting and the wife of one intervenes to save her husband from the blows of his opponent, if she stretches out her hand and seizes the latter by his private parts, you shall chop off her hand without pity.** (Dt 25:11-12)

Schooled as we are in respect for Sacred Scripture as the inspired Word of God, it is hardly unfair to ask, "Could not the All-Wise, All-Merciful, All-Loving God of Israel have come up with something more God-like than this?" Our answer must take the following facts into consideration.

The divine inspiration we correctly attribute to Old Testament scripture need not necessarily imply divine *finality* in any statement or concept. That is, the overall theme of Old Testament literature reflects the gradual progressive disclosure of God to His people through His actions in their history. The Lord's plan for self-Revelation appears always in the Old Testament as a widening, deepening one. Since God in essence is Mystery, and mystery by religious definition *inexhaustible truth,* there is a fundamental dynamism—a continuous journey-of-penetration-into-the-Unknown quality about the ancient Scripture. Naturally, from our perspective in the New Dispensation we can look back upon instances of God's manifestation in Israel's history and recognize them as "consciousness-raising" events. For they apparently are designed to elevate preparedness for that point in space and time when the divine and human would meet in absolute conjunction.

**Entitled with scholarly equanimity in the *Jerusalem Bible* edition "modesty in brawls"(!)

For instance, mind-expanding progression in Revelation may be traced from the initial divine call to Abraham to bring a new tribe into existence. The next "step" occurs as God's call to Moses results in freedom and a new identity as a nation for Israel. Only at this advanced stage of preparedness does the Lord "localize" His call in specifically *moral* terms with the presentation of the Law to Moses on Sinai. Logically, the confidence of the Israelites in God's power to deliver and preserve them physically would precede the extension of their trust in His power to save—and rule—morally and spiritually.**

God demonstrates that He works *through* as well as *in* history. The Lord formed the fledgling nation of Israel from nomadic clans roaming the northwest Arabian desert at the opening of the Bronze Age. Understandably, Israel's early comprehension of her God and His ways would be commensurate with the primitive development of culture and the limited level of human awareness available to men at that time. In addition, the rough-hewn "martial law" aspects of Mosaic Law may not seem so cruel or unusual when one considers Israel's critical need for rigorous internal discipline. Beset by powerful, hostile neighbors, her sheer survival demanded stringent measures that would confirm a sense of tribal identity and facilitate a strict sense of authority and obedience. Nor should we ignore the important advances Levitical and Deuteronomic Law made in elevating Israelite morality above the level of the jungle. While "eye for eye

---

** The New Testament offers an excellent example of such divine efforts to elicit human faith in the episode of Jesus confronted by the Pharisees while dealing with a paralytic. Challenged to prove his power to forgive sins, Jesus declares "which is easier to say, 'Your sins are forgiven' or 'Stand up and walk!' He then substantiates his claim to accomplish the *unseen* (i.e., forgive sins) by a preliminary display of visible, physical healing. (Luke 5:17-26).

and tooth for tooth" may strike us as simply a crude call for vengeance and unbridled violence, we fail to appreciate the *limits* just such a dictum set upon older, still more violent precedents. Primitive peoples, recall, were not always willing to settle for "eye for eye" retribution. Injustice done to one member of a certain tribe might spark wholesale annihilation of a rival clan. In this respect, the unlimited warfare bloodbaths horrifyingly common to the "modern age" bespeak much less moral refinement than was displayed by the desert-dwelling Israelites some thirteen centuries before Christ.

Israel was born—and remained through the peaks and valleys of her history—a thoroughgoing *theocracy*. Hence "justice" or "righteousness" was interpreted in the collective conscience of the Chosen People as a God-centered rather than man-centered value. This meant that the Law was predicated not on such general humanitarian criteria as "common decency," "simple equity," "tolerant fairmindedness," etc., but upon what Israel believed to be the *will of God for her*. Thus while the Law does respect some commonly accepted personal prerogatives, and shows numerous instances of great-heartedness, the contemporary notion of "natural law" rights and responsibilities is not at all central to its considerations. Israel sees herself as *belonging to God*, and the Law speaks to Israel as His voice.

The story of Abraham and his son Isaac (Gn 22:1-19) illustrates this lesson as well as anything in the Old Testament (and in fact says more about the *essence* of morality in the ancient Scripture than do the Ten Commandments). God demands of Abraham the sacrifice of his son. Having abandoned his land, relinquished his freedom (placing himself at God's disposal), and even accepted a new "name" and thus a new identity as a person, Abraham is virtually asked to surrender his very manhood. Few crimes could match the brutalization of psyche inherent in the slaying of a son. All human instincts rebel against such a thing. To obey God's command means the destruction of Isaac, and most likely, of Abraham himself spiritually. To resist the Almighty implies the suffering of unnamed but assuredly terrible consequences. At length, for better or worse, Abraham casts his lot with a God Who orders filicide.

As we know, the tale climaxes in a "happy" resolution as Abraham's sacrificial hand is stayed at the last instant and Isaac is saved. But this upbeat conclusion to the "testing" of Abraham is the least consequential part of the story. As any child of the Covenant would be quick to learn, Abraham's decision to renounce both reason and emotion in favor of faith is the central moral lesson.

This episode reinforces the vote of "no confidence" that Genesis levies on the moral aptitude of post-Fall man. Here Abraham makes a hard choice in favor of the God Whose ways are clearly not man's ways, and that choice is lauded in the Scripture. A pedantic essay on the extremes of the "leap" to faith could hardly hope to equal the impact of this little drama. In it are summarized the twin pillars of Old Testament moral theology: "right" and "wrong" are not products of human intuition but disclosures through divine revelation; and, God's call for reconciliation with all men begins with a summons to His special People: be re-created in the spirit of faith and in the "flesh" of the Law.

Chapter III

A New Creation:
The Moral Spirit of the New Testament

The Davidic Period (roughly 1010-970 B.C.) brought a united Israel to the zenith of its power as a kingdom. Administrative efficiency became more important to the orderly conduct of government over the extensive Palestinian region, and as a result the traditions of the Mosaic Law which had been handed down orally for over three centuries were collected and set down in writing. In the almost 1000 years that intervened between that time and the birth of Jesus in Bethlehem, the spiritual consciousness of Israel became woven cocoon-like around the sacred prescriptions of the ancient Law.

No faithful Israelite doubted that the Law stood as God's own Covenant binding Him to the holy nation which traced its bloodlines to the seed of Abraham. The Law made possible that unique communion of religious observance, social custom, and political convention that characterized the People God chose to be His own. The illumination of human behavior as the focal point of the God-man relationship was among its chief features. The Law voiced an unmistakable invitation to goodness that required the positive response of men's deeds.

The very fact of our Christian religious belief shows that we esteem the Old Covenant as divinely inspired. At the same time we recognize that it is neither the *last* Word in revealed moral teaching, nor the finalized embodiment of the Lord's "good news" to man. God's ultimate Word of peace and reconciliation remained to be spoken.

The Old Law established a new "ground" for dialogue between God and man, but it did not revive all the conditions of *interpersonal rapprochement* that Genesis mythologized in the Garden of Eden. Nor as God's Word was it always received at the address intended—the conscientious life-center of the "heart." Time and again the Lord found it necessary to raise up *Prophets*, assigning them the grueling task of preaching *internal* conversion to those who found scrupulous, selective observance of the Law's *letter* a conveniently self-serving device for escaping the challenge of its spirit.

Finally, for all its scope and wordy attention to detail, the Old Law was basically conservative in its ambitions. It sought to do little more than to glorify God's transcendence while thwarting man's idolatrous tendencies toward fatal pride. In its application the Law functioned more to contain or repress the worst in man than to wring from him inspiring examples of his virtue at its best.

What was the attitude of Jesus—Son of God *and* son of Abraham—to the Law? The Gospels suggest Jesus was respectful toward the Old Covenant, but able to see and act beyond its limits. To the rich young man who seeks counsel on how to "possess everlasting life," Jesus first cites observance of the Decalogue as fundamental. He adds, however, that *perfection* (a key concept of Jesus' ethical teaching) demands more of a person than the Law prescribes. (Mt 19: 16-22).

THE MESSIAH AND THE KINGDOM

> Do not suppose that my mission on earth is to spread peace. My mission is to spread, not peace but division . . . to make a man's enemies those of his own household . . . He who will not take up his cross and follow me is not worthy of me. (Mt 10:34, 36-37)

The Bringer of *God's* Peace, Unity, and Reconciliation is not about to permit reduction of their meaning to Rotarian good-fellowship terms. We see something of the divine jealousy that guarded the purity of the Lord's works from human corruption in the Old Testament flare again in the prophetic posture of Jesus. He refuses to shrink from controversy. He beards the Pharisees in their own bailiwick with charges of corruption and hypocrisy. The crowds which flatter him with adulation turn against him surprised and frustrated at his rejection of a demagogue's role. The Synoptic Evangelists reveal the substance of Jesus' mission as the proclamation of the Kingdom—the New Reign of God—and his determination to prevent that Kingdom from being misconstrued either as a worldly political empire or a totally other-worldly phantasm. The gift Jesus brings *is* peace—but not as "the world" has known or imagined it. It is, rather, the unified "life to the full" experienced by those willing to drink with him from the "same cup" (Mt 20:23) and to be bathed in the self-sacrificial "Blood of The Lamb" (Rv 7:14).

Addressed to a Jewish audience conversant with the promises of the Covenant and the sacredness of the Law, Matthew's Gospel aims to show the fulfillment of both in the "New Moses"—Jesus Christ. "You have heard the commandment imposed on your forefathers . . . [but] what I say to you is:" Repeated several times in the fifth chapter of Matthew, this formula represents Jesus' claim to "speak with authority" in the matter of revealed divine moral law. As part of the "Evangelical Discourse" (the great "Sermon on the Mount") this important selection teaches that Jesus would have his followers move beyond the Old Testament concept of "righteousness" (*justice*) as the basis for human relationships. The ideal that Jesus preaches and lives is *perfection* and the key to its understanding as well as its practice is *love*.

If Matthew is the "educator"—painstakingly documenting evidence of Old Testament expectation fulfilled in the Christ Event—Mark might be labeled "the Pamphleteer." Most likely the earliest of the Gospels to be compiled, and surely the most "primitive" in the terms of brevity and abruptness of style, Mark teaches us of the Kingdom's coming by letting Jesus' actions speak for themselves. Like Matthew, Mark sees Jesus in the context of his Messianic mission as herald of the new and enduring Reign of God. Mark is even more attentive to the efforts Jesus makes to deflect public attention from himself as author of miraculous works, preferring to leaven the public consciousness with hints of a more ponderous entrance of God's power in the spiritual lives of all men. In the so-called "messianic secret" passages of Mark (e.g., 1:44; 3:12; 7:36) Jesus bids those he cures and even demons he expels to remain silent about the effects of divine power they have felt.

Mark's Gospel, however, is neither silent nor ambiguous about the meaning of the Reign of God as it is revealed in and through Jesus. With a keen sense of the disintegrating breakdown suffered by man and nature as described in the Fall account of Genesis, Mark sees in Jesus the reconstructive, healing power of God overshadowing the world once more. The signs of God's re-conquest of the world from the forces of darkness and chaos are posted as victories over the brute savagery of nature in the quelling of the storm, over physical infirmities, over demonic affliction, over spiritual enslavement in forgiving the paralytic's sins, and even over man's most formidable enemy, death itself, in the raising of the daughter of Jairus. In a passage some Scripture scholars feel is deliberately reminiscent of Gn 1:31, "God looked at everything he had made, and he found it very good," Mark salutes the magnificent re-creative acts of Jesus with the spontaneous laudatory exclamation of the crowds: "He has done everything well!" (7:37).

Mark's Gospel thunders with a martial air. Its tones are heavy with the decisive beat of God's footsteps marching in the person of the "Son of Man" against the tyranny of evil enslaving creation. By comparison the Gospel of Luke addresses the theme of Redemptive reconciliation from a higher, more light-hearted register. Luke's is referred to as the "Gospel of the Holy Spirit" since it celebrates the blossoming of the latent Spirit of God in hearts warmed by the presence of Christ. Luke, the perceptive historian, is the most "person-centered" of the Evangelists. From His "birth among shepherds" to His "death between thieves," Jesus' life in Luke unfolds as the story of "the man for others." Luke pays particular attention to the distress of the sinner, and in the parables of the lost sheep, the finding of the lost coin, and the prodigal son, he dramatizes the eagerness of God in His loving kindness to extend mercy and to welcome the repentant.

Scholars date Luke's Gospel around A.D. 80. There is good reason to assume that its theology responds to certain transitional developments in the early Church. Through the decades immediately following Jesus' death many disciples held fervent hopes of His impending return in glory to inaugurate the Messianic Kingdom. As years moved on, however, without the appearance of Christ in his Second Coming, the Christian community was forced to reappraise its expectations in the light of faith. With its emphasis on the perpetual presence of the Holy Spirit among all who accept the Lordship of Christ, Luke's Gospel (and its complementary sequel *The Acts of The Apostles*) builds on the understanding that the Kingdom *has arrived* in Christ, and that the *fullness* of its coming must be preceded by the active efforts of believers to live Christ's life in their own. Luke's is a theology that stresses emulation of Christ by participation in the social process. The missionary character of the Church gains reinforcement from the extensive coverage Luke assigns Christ's "sending of the seventy-two" in the 10th chapter. As exemplified in the famous Good Samaritan parable, the Christian is responsible for substantiating his faith by laboring even as Jesus did to bind up human wounds and repair the hurts of nature. Luke sees zeal for participation in the reconciling action of Christ as essential for the authentic believer. To those who recognize the Samaritan as the true "neighbor," Luke quotes Jesus' pointed reply: "Then go and do the same." (10:37).

ONENESS IN CHRIST: LIFE TO THE FULL

When one examines the four Gospel accounts it is interesting to note that preoccupation with the *earliest* events in the story of Christ's coming increases in proportion to the *lateness* of the particular account. Thus we find, for instance, that Mark—probably the earliest Gospel to appear after Jesus' death—contains neither an infancy account nor a genealogy. No attention is paid in Mark to Jesus' early personal life or to his ancestry. Infancy narratives appear in both Matthew and Luke. Significantly, the genealogy in Matthew traces the lineage of Jesus back to the Patriarch Abraham— Father of the Chosen People. As a vehicle for identifying Jesus as Savior of *all* men, the more universalist record of Luke includes a genealogy that links Jesus by descendancy all the way back to *Adam*.

The Gospel of John, most likely the latest of the books (dating probably from A.D. 90-100), and the most theologically stylized and reflective of the Gospel accounts, dispenses with both genealogy and infancy narratives. In its unique Prologue, however, the Gospel of John notes as the "origins" of Jesus His very infinite pre-existence as Christ in God. "In the beginning was the Word. . ." The Word (*Logos*) in John's theological understanding represents the *creative power* of God; the action that alone calls into being all that is. The Gospel of John recounts the enfleshment of that Word in the person of Jesus, and it portrays His mission as one of finalizing the creative action of His Father. This He accomplishes by baptizing all who believe in Him in His own Holy Spirit; that is, in the "living water" of eternal life.

The action of Jesus as seen through the eyes of John is uniquely one of "nativitizing"; of *creating* in the most authentic sense of *bringing to birth*. "I have life because of the Father," Jesus tells his followers (6:57), explaining that even as He derives life-sustaining nourishment from doing His Father's will, so all who "(feed) on my flesh and (drink) my blood" (6:54), all who make themselves one with the Lord Jesus will discover the incarnate life of the Spirit of God welling-up and developing irreversibly within them.

John's Gospel reveals Jesus as the Son to Whom has been entrusted the task of reconciling men with each other and unifying them—through Himself—with their Father. Importantly, He instructs His disciples that, having experienced rebirth to new life in the Spirit, they must not be content to live a dehumanized, non-incarnational existence in the world. They too must participate in the creative action of bringing to birth new life in others. To emphasize this point the Johannine account of the Last Supper substitutes the *washing of the feet* for the Eucharistic institution narrative contained in the Synoptic writings. Having arisen from the table,

Jesus bathes the feet of his surprised and embarrassed apostles. In his final "sign" to them before the Crucifixion, he teaches that they must be servants of the Spirit struggling to come alive in the hearts of men. By pledging faith in Christ his followers have put off the deadening production-consumption ethos of "the world." For those who have taken to their hearts the life-giving Spirit of Truth there must be a sign of their commitment.

THE NEW LAW OF LOVE

This is how all will know you for my disciples:
your love for one another. (Jn 13:35)

The "farewell discourse" that runs from the 13th through the 17th chapters of John crystallizes the teaching of Jesus that man discovers others, fulfills himself, and encounters God not in the Law but in love.

The English word "love" must bear the burden of many and varying degrees of meaning ("I love . . . my work . . . my wife . . . a fast game of tennis . . . a hot bath . . ."). The Greek from which the New Testament comes down to us differentiates by three terms the characteristics we usually identify with "love." The first, *eros*, refers to that kind of "love" in which a subject is attracted to an object because of the object's inherent goodness or beauty or desirability. In common parlance the term "erotic" has sexual overtones. But in its classical form *eros* describes that gravitation toward anything—a pretty face, a work of art, a chocolate cake— possessed of qualities that appeal to us. No "response" on the part of the attracting object is necessary for the erotic form of love to exist in the admiring subject.

A second mode of "love" distinguished by the Greeks is *philia* (cf. *Phila*delphia—"City of Brotherly Love"). This refers to a relationship between two subjects arising from mutual need or common dependency. Philia exists where something would be lacking in each subject if it were not for the other.

The final, most noble love form categorized by the Greeks is *agape*. Perhaps best translated as "absolute" or "unconditional benevolence," *agape* exists where a subject supports or relates to another subject out of pure gratuity. No inherent attractiveness is required on the other's part, nor any condition of mutual support, nor even any stipulation of reciprocity. *Agape* stands for a love relationship of constancy maintained by a subject regardless of whether the other responds positively, negatively, or indifferently to it.

The God to Whom Jesus relates and Whom he emulates is pure *Agape;* the love-active, unconditionally benevolent *Father*. It is clear enough to Jesus that he shares the intimacy of a father-son relationship with the God Whom he addresses in prayer. But for many of his listeners accustomed to the ancient conceptualizations of their Lord as Omnipotent Judge, Law-Giver, and Transcendent Nation-Builder the possibility of such tenderness and familiarity between man and God is utterly astounding. To the amazement of his listeners and to the scandal of the religious establishment of Israel Jesus openly professes blood-union with the Almighty Ancient of Days. "The Father and I are one." But if this bond destines Jesus for future glory, it also marks him for the consequences of total self-giving. For the sign of absolute unity with the *agape* of the Father is life-unto-death for the world that the Father has made.

Through his humanity Jesus obviously enjoys an authentic unity with all who are human. At one and the same time he draws into himself the singular God-life of *agape* and the human existence common to each of us. Since then the Old Testament has revealed human behavior (morality) to be the standard currency of exchange between God and man, the life style of Jesus becomes of itself a message-conveying medium. That life demonstrates the practical living-out of God's life in the situation of one man, and it becomes an active-statement (*Word*) shouted from the rooftops proclaiming that the Fallen state of man need not be his final one. As St. Paul explains it, the slavery to sin and death which was every man's sentence even under the dispensation of the Old Law gives way to the victory of *agape* in Christ. The Resurrection of Jesus ("first born from the dead") signals the triumph of love-in-God over the strongest of the forces of darkness.

The "good news," then, is that all persons are truly *graced* in Christ. That is, the gift Jesus imparts to each of us is the potential for living in God—even as he lived it to perfection first. What we must remember, though, as St. Paul rebukingly reminded the Corinthian Christians, is that the Redemptive victory of Christ makes it *possible* for us to live the God-life fruitfully. It is no "cheap grace" substitute for efforts along that line on our part.

THE "LOVE-LIFE" OF THE CHRISTIAN: A SIGN AND A SACRIFICE

When St. Paul made the drastic course-change in life that led him into the "New Way" of Christ, he brought with him the tools he developed as a rabbinic zealot: a perceptive eye and a sharp tongue for religious abuses. He was quick to notice that the seeds of an imbalanced theology of the Paschal Mystery were bearing bad fruit in certain improprieties and excesses of early Christian Eucharistic gatherings. Condemning the tendency to view the Eucharist narrowly as an occasion given over exclusively to euphoric (and sometimes debauched) merriment at the Resurrection event, Paul emphasized the *sacrificial* character of this central act of worship (cf. 1 Cor 11:17-34). His criticism was not intended to diminish the fundamentally joyful, hopeful nature of the Eucharist. Nor was Paul interested in reducing this Sacrament of Redemption to a dour recitation of man's shameful complicity in the agonies of the Passion. Rather, he called attention in a positive way to the solemn bond—the New Covenant—that Jesus initiated with his followers at the Last Supper. The faithful who commemorate that meal not only make credal assent to the fact of Jesus' Resurrection, they also bind themselves ritually to the Lord at precisely the moment when he prepares to make offering to his Father of all he has to give.

> Every time then, you eat this bread and drink this cup, you proclaim the death of the Lord until he comes! (1 Cor 11:26)

The death that Paul speaks of is not limited to the bloody Crucifixion event, but is meant to encompass the lifelong act of Jesus' self-outpouring (*kenosis*) for the world. Practically speaking, then, to "die with Christ" means to live freely and fully with him for the good of others. Since Jesus is at one with the Father Whose very Being is pure *agape* (constant outpouring in love), the sign of our reconciliation with that same heavenly Father is the dimension of outpouring *our* lives take on in union with the gift of the Son.

Paul's ability to perceive doctrinal mystery blossoming into liturgical expression, and in turn flowing evenly and richly into daily living experience is proof of his immense spiritual stature. The lessons his vision can teach are very urgently needed by the Christian "hungering and thirsting" for an integral experience of Word, worship, and Kingdom-advancing moral "work" today.

A good deal of that lesson can be learned by carefully tracing the development of Paul's thought from the 11th through the 14th chapters of his First Letter to the Corinthians. There his treatment of the unity-sign of sacramental Eucharist leads into remarks on the Christian's responsibility to discern the Real Presence of Christ and the gifts of His

Holy Spirit in the personal "members" of his Whole Body. This intricate tapestry interweaving Christian spiritual, sacramental, and moral life ranks among the most outstanding segments of the Pauline *corpus,* and it includes a masterpiece of elegant simplicity—the 13th Chapter paean to love.

Essentially, love as revealed in all of New Testament Scripture amounts to action against estrangement. It is the gravitational force ultimately integrating the human personality and enlivening the human community. The Kingdom of God Jesus proclaims and the *perfection* to which he summons his hearers are situations of *wholeness* made real by the presence of Divine love. The Gospels record Jesus' dealings with many kinds of persons displaying a variety of attitudes and problems. In every case the *agape* that is his by nature reveals itself in the consistent appeal Christ makes to the other's undying potential for good.

In the Master's eyes no one he meets, however deeply they may be corroded by sin or scarred by self-rejection, is without at least a spark of responsiveness to the outreach of another who sincerely cares. Layers of defensiveness (hostility, inferiority, insecurity, etc.) may intervene to block that spark from being fanned. But time and again Jesus demonstrates the power genuine love has to penetrate even to the most thoroughly imprisoned hearts. This he does by opening himself to those most obviously troubled, convincing them that he poses no threat, that he cares for them, has regard for their feelings, understanding for their fears or their anguish, and most of all is interested in their happiness. Jesus makes no compromise with evil, yet he makes clear his determination to build upon the strengths—not belittle or condemn the weaknesses—of those he finds in need.

Since *agape* is truly dynamic God-life available to man, Jesus embraces it as the creative force which alone can bring real transformation to the sinful or despairing soul. Of course, *agape*—true, selfless love—renders one vulnerable to considerable suffering. Because it is unconditioned upon the response of the other, *agape* calls for the risk of injury or rejection at the hands of the other, while remaining dedicated to the other's welfare. As the Gospels show us in the life of Christ, suffering the attacks of another without returning person-destroying malice in kind *is* a real human possibility. Yet it is a powerful challenge.

Sacrifice of self is an inevitability for the authentic Christian. This does not imply, however, that the true Christian indulges in masochism nor does he give himself over to the blows of the world with a Stoic's insensateness. Rather, the Christian follows the Lord who believed, lived, and taught that evil returned for evil is merely the escalation of destruction and non-being. *Transformation* of the other can evolve only through a commitment to respect the dignity inherent in the other, and this demands a refusal to harm him simply for spite or vengeance. To accept evil from others while steadfastly persisting to do them *good* is the most powerful example of conviction in a meaning to life that transcends mere ego-gratification. Such witness has the energy to transform and convert the offender. It also leaves the Christian "powerless" in worldly terms. It amounts, as St. Paul observes, to "the folly of the Cross."

Summing up our sketchy overview of the "New Creation" in Christ as the New Testament presents it, let's say this. If we consider Jesus purely as one among many of history's notable "religious leaders," his life and teaching need not seem all that unique. If, however, our reading of the Gospels is informed by faith, we know him to be the One Who takes to himself all that it is to be man, all that it is to be God. If once, then, in the continuum of Revelation we could point to the *Law* of the Old Covenant as a crossroads of the divine and the human, we now recognize a new and thoroughly revolutionary point of contact with the Lord God. Conceptually, the original model

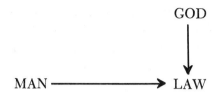

has given way to the final, grand act of reconciliation in which the God Who is Love embraces forever the Son—Who is One with us.

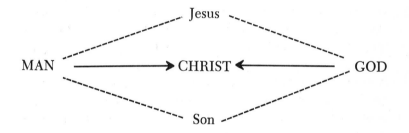

Chapter IV

A Modern Look at Sin and Forgiveness

CONFESSION AND THE SENSE OF SIN

We have described Christ's *Way* as life lived in *agape*, growth in unconditioned acceptance of and care for others. Yet as we all know from experience, our growth is often irregular and imperfect. Since free will permits us to opt for the harmful as well as the beneficial, the superficially attractive as well as the genuinely good for others and ourselves, we each need opportunities for "quality control" review of our living patterns. Penance offers the Christian believer a major sacramental grace-point for constructive self-criticism in light of the Gospel ideal.

When penitent and confessor are both well prepared to engage each other reverently and thoughtfully, the healing, life-giving powers of the Sacrament can play through an orchestral range of themes and variations. The Sacrament itself stands for the unlimited (". . . seventy times seven times") willingness of God to forgive. It is always available for the sincerely repentant. The Sacrament of Penance displaces fear of God's wrath with the reassurance that we ". . . are worth more than many sparrows" (Mt 10:31) to our Loving Father. We have the chance to face our sinfulness, to ponder the distortion it brings to our personhood, admit the harm it causes our neighbor, and openly disavow its hold on our lives by invoking God's merciful grace. Through personal conscience examination, prayerful reflection, and dialogue with the confessor, the Sacrament makes it possible for us to develop the most promising strategies for personal interior renewal. It should also deepen our awareness of responsibility for social extension of our Christian witness. Penance has the power to free us from enslavement to the "old man" of our past, increase sensitivity to our role in Christ's Present, and motivate our preparedness to receive His Kingdom as it awaits us in the future.

The action Christ begins in us through Penance is reconciliation. It is a healing of the broken or disjointed, a mending of the torn, a rebuilding of the defaced. We are called away from the age-old disharmony of "flesh and spirit" that we label today as "anxiety," "alienation," or "estrangement." When we hold up to ourselves the mirror of self-evaluation in the Sacrament of Penance, the returning image should outline us as we really are, not as we would pretend to be for the world. And since the features we examine there are often found to be disfigured by our passions (money, sex, power, status, etc.) or by the cosmetic phoniness of our falsehood to others, the Sacrament stimulates us to rid ourselves of this ugliness.

Change for the better begins as we open to the reality of God's forgiveness, calling on us as it does to accept *His* image in our lives as the very best of our own. Reconciliation with our Father is well under way when we can confront ourselves and others, convinced that what we perceive in the viewing captures something of God's Self-image: acceptable, appealing, and precious.

Penance is *meant* to be a well-integrated symphony of grace. It should echo with the renewed harmony of peace with oneself, with others, and with God. Quite frankly, however, the Saturday-afternoon-in-the-confessional-box experience common to most Catholics seems sadly anemic as a heartfelt rite of conversion and reconciliation. For though most penitents are well-schooled in the "Bless me, Father..." verbal forms and precise number-and-species categorization of offenses, too few seem aware that confessing means more than the telling, and forgiveness more than the dismissing of their faults.

"Perhaps the greatest sin of our age is the loss of the sense of sin." Pope Pius XII made that statement in the early 1940's and it remains eminently relevant today. Moreover it provides an excellent starting point for a look at some of the problems besetting Penance in the contemporary Church.

First, to suggest that we have lost "the sense of sin" is to do more than engage in the kind of pious handwringing over the "universal breakdown in morality" that surfaces in the sermonizing of virtually every age. What we are concerned with is the discovery that the devout frequent penitent who (in all good faith) recites in confession the same time-worn "grocery list" of peccadillos may well have lost as much "sense of sin" as the most flagrant and callous serious sinner. One reason for this may well be the kind of catechesis on sin that a number of generations have grown up with.

Stated simply, there has in the past been too strong an emphasis on *sins*—conceptualized quantitatively and discontinuously—while insufficient attention has been paid to *sin* as a pervasive, ever-present force tending toward the distortion of truth and destruction of good in personal and social life.

Youngsters learning about evil, and congregations listening to sermons on it have been handed a conceptual framework top-heavy in stress upon identifying *occasions* of mortal or venial *actual sins*. The enumeration of offenses ("... angry three times, disobedient five times, uncharitable in speech twice, etc.") has thus come across to many Catholics as the quintessence of Sacramental confession. As a result, pre-confession examination of conscience has, for large numbers of penitents, settled into an "isolation booth" test of total numerical recall. Too little encouragement has been given penitents to *analyze* underlying *causes* of behavior confessed (*why* did I become angry with *this* person at *this* time? what does this tell me about the conditions under which I'm most likely to become provoked? what positive steps should I be taking to avoid reacting this way in the future?). Mental restriction to the "numbers game" conscience review has also hindered penitents from developing the ability to see confession matter in terms of longer-range styles or patterns of living, rather than merely as isolated, discontinuous events.

For example, a housewife may find herself repeatedly confessing numerous instances of "impatience with the children." She does so because she has come to assume that such moments of emotional rise or upset are sinful. Yet a bit of gentle questioning by the confessor will reveal: (1) that she never thought to conceive of this "impatience" in context of her role as loving disciplinarian and order-keeper in the home, subject to the pressures of her demanding task, and relating to children rather than to mature adults; or (2) even if there is some legitimate element of culpability present, she has given no consideration to ways-and-means of changing or modifying an unsatisfactory behavior pattern in herself.

While some may find it trifling to reflect more thoughtfully on the "venial" matter we confess, and others may even see in it an unhealthy movement toward the "rationalizing away" of sin, penitents deserve instruction and encouragement in efforts to grow toward deeper, more mature self-examination. For laxity in cultivating a meaningful "sense of sin" can result in the penitent's drifting away toward a self-satisfied, unholy complacency; or, in the opposite direction, toward a spiritual depression or even despair.

Applied to the case of the "impatient housewife" this might mean reaching a decision that the constant repetition of this "fault" was proving embarrassing, demeaning, or simply boring to her. With no real relief from this undesired burden of impatience evolving from its mere repeated appearance in the litany of confessed matter, the penitent may begin to feel serious doubts about the efficacy of the Sacrament's grace. Consequently, the penitent may begin to reason that if a particular fault invariably recurs whenever the conscience is examined (and the fault per se is acknowledged *not* to be gravely sinful in nature), a simple face-saving device is to confess less and less frequently. In other words, since going to confession is not helping me *stop* doing what I'm ashamed of, then at least I'm bound to feel less uneasy if I simply minimize the number of occasions I make use of confession and have to face my perpetual failure in this particular area.

Of course, another common but opposite reaction to an inability to break out of such a behavior pattern is merely to *accept* its inevitability, ignore any call of conscience to change the pattern, and rely solely on the frequent confessing of the fault as a protective "umbrella" shielding one against the danger of any "fallout" of God's displeasure. This is to reduce a loving encounter with the forgiving Christ to a ritual game-playing with an apparently whimsical God Who seems more interested in exacting appeasement from His bumbling subjects than bestowing mercy upon His Holy People.

PENITENTIAL CONVERSION AND ORIGINAL SIN

An enlightened "sense of sin" requires us to know more about it than the species-and-number quantifiers tell us. Certainly we must be able to point out specific occasions on which we have acted contrary to God's Will. Yet a real entering into reconciliation with the Father presupposes that we have dealt with evil as a profoundly mysterious element of the human condition. Confessing our complicity in it demands that we see more to it than individual, self-contained units of wrongdoing piling up like cold cut slices that fall from a whirling meat cutter.

Undoubtedly there was at least a strong subconscious impulse in the minds of many who flocked to see *The Exorcist* to pin the source of evil down to mentally-manageable terms. The villain in that recent box office sensation was, of course, a demon. But horrifying as its depiction was in that motion picture, the demon provided a certain aesthetic satisfaction. Though invisible the demon was quite obviously *there;* a *persona* at which the audience could point and say "Ah, evil. *That* is what you are!"

Real life robs us of the dubious satisfaction of delimiting sin in space or time. At its core evil defies man's understanding as *Job*, that literary and theological masterpiece of Old Testament wisdom tells us. When all is said and done in *Job*, evil remains beyond man's ken, and is in itself a rebuke to man's pride.

Conversion is the act of personal passover to freedom. If sacramental confession plays a major part in this liberation process it must enable us to reach beyond the surface *expressions* of our attachment to the unholy (that is, our *actual sins*), putting us in contact with something of the deeper mystery of evil that binds us in error, fear, and self-centeredness to the "old man" in each of us. In more categorical terms, our procedures for conscience examination and preparation for prayerful dialogue in the Sacrament of Penance must take greater account of the effects of *original sin*.

Meeting in the 16th century, the Council of Trent sought

to clarify and standardize the rites for administration of the sacraments. In the aftermath of the Reformation there was great need for articulating simple, precise formulas governing dogma and liturgy. It was from Trent that the confession of "species and number" of sins was declared to be an integral part of the form for the Sacrament of Penance. At the same time the Tridentine Council Fathers reaffirmed that the confessional matter of actual sin had roots in the moral infirmity of man defined by the term "effects of original sin."

The doctrine of original sin—certainly among the most fascinating insights into man's situation to emerge from Sacred Scripture—has unfortunately been victimized and somewhat emasculated over the centuries by the treatment it has received in catechetics and apologetics. While it might have been used to advantage as bed-rock for a solid, popular theology of Penance (illuminating that Sacrament as a response to the mystery of evil in creation), doctrine on original sin has instead been trotted out almost exclusively for purposes of apologetically justifying infant baptism. Consequently, teaching on original sin has been filtered through pulpit and catechism only in the skeletal, abstract outline of five main points:

1) Related to the sin of Adam, original sin constitutes a pre-existing condition of alienation from God into which all persons are born;

2) Original sin is inherited (rather than merited by positive culpability);

3) It deprives one of complete (heavenly) union with God;

4) Baptism cleanses the soul of original sin;

5) Yet, original sin's "effects" of weakness before temptation and the deprivation of the "preternatural gifts" remain as constants.

For many Catholics the idea of "original sin" carries no

real weight. It is easily dismissed as "something taken away by Baptism." But if it can be seen in light of some contemporary moral questions and applied to some experience common to everyday practical living, not only is it possible for us to grow in a more mature understanding of *sin*, but of the sign-value of Baptism and Penance as well.

Let us say that original sin means basically this: that each of us at birth must enter a real world filled with ambiguity. It is a world possessed of evil as well as good; weighed down by sin although filled with grace; woefully ignorant and yet crammed with knowledge; bathed in sorrow while wealthy in joy; wracked by hatred but abundant in love.

Further, let us remind ourselves that our lifespan on the average will not exceed the Biblical "threescore years and ten." Scientists estimate that some 100 billion human beings have trod the earth since the race of man began, and most have lived within the maximum span of a single century.

Quite obviously, the moment in history, the civilization, the society, the culture, the class, the community, neighborhood and family into which one is born will all influence his development as a person. Likewise the prevailing ideas and ideals of his time: the myths, beliefs, attitudes, values, goals, philosophies and fears that shape the concepts through which he frames the "real world" will be handed to him largely from sources outside himself.

Truly no one of us is an island. The raw material that goes into shaping our rational and emotional, conscious and subconscious existence begins flowing through our being even in its pre-natal stages and continues throughout life. Because our physical senses are programmed to assimilate as much as they can of the world outside us, invariably much of what we funnel in as the unrefined ore of our judgments and concepts will be limited, slanted, corrupted, unhealthy, false. Naturally, the end "product" of our ideas will be an alloy stamped out of weaker and stronger component ingredients.

When we say, then, that original sin is "inherited weakness" we mean that the imperfect world prevailing around us envelops and to some extent morally debilitates us prior to any culpable act on our part. As the colorfully trenchant Old Testament passage has it:

> The fathers have eaten unripe grapes, and the children's teeth are set on edge. (Ezk 18:2; Jr 31:29)

At this point, let us turn to a practical example of such inherited moral debility. Say a society for some reason finds it expedient to discriminate against a minority group on the basis of race. Down through numerous generations that society permits social, cultural, and legal powers to reinforce the myth of racial inequality. Children growing up within that society—children of both oppressed and oppressing races —will interiorize that myth and act out their social roles accordingly. The majority race child will be conditioned to perpetuate the superiority myth and be equipped with the tools of domination. The minority race child, encountering the structures of the dominant society and observing the limitations imposed on "his kind," will early in life begin assimilating convictions of his own inferiority.

Neither child was responsible for the origination of the myth. Neither has any real chance to avoid its influence. Both are left handicapped by it.

Ironically, many of the same staunch church-going Christians who would assent unreservedly to the abstract "5 point" dogmatic formula on original sin would prove highly resentful at the suggestion that as white, middle-class Americans one probable, practical manifestation of original sin in *their* lives is at least a subconscious tainting of racism.

In other words, most of us do not object to "fessing up" with Flip Wilson that "the devil made me do it" when it comes to acknowledging our minor failings and peccadilloes. But when it comes to considering that some of our sacrosanct ideological ideals, social standards, and cultural totems may be flawed with the residue of an "original sin," open-heartedness faces its most demanding trial. For in addition to being inadvertently "lost," the *sense of sin* may also be deliberately abandoned.

BAPTISM AND PENANCE—SIGNS OF VICTORY IN THE STRUGGLE FOR NEW LIFE

The doctrine on original sin would print out on a graph like a parabolic curve. The nadir—the curve's lowest segment—would mark the point at which the doctrine teaches that we all inherit from the sinful past a legacy of error that obstructs our accomplishment of the good in the present. But our bondage to the past need not remain total nor permanent. Baptism in Jesus Christ provides impetus for an upswing toward hope on our graph of human destiny.

It is important that when we speak of the "efficacy" of Baptism—that is, what the sacrament really *does* for us in regard to original sin—we must guard against oversimplifying or "mechanizing" its action. Too often we have allowed ourselves to regard the sacraments much like spiritual filling stations, one-stop service facilities entirely self-contained and limited in scope to a few moments of formal ritual activity.

The sacramental grace of Baptism which breaks the bond of original sin must reach out in time and space far beyond the moment of the sacrament's infant conferral. As the doctrine on original sin teaches, genuine freedom to see and do the good *is* possible. But the channels for its grace must continue to flow with an on-going education in the faith and an ever-deepening commitment to the Christ-life on the part of the baptized.

We mentioned above some of the damaging "cultural conditioning" factors that propagate original sin, adding that we feel the effects of such sin in the attractiveness or appeal that evil holds out for us. Yet however strongly pre-conditioned we may be to accept sin-laden myth, we believe in faith that to proclaim Jesus Christ as *Savior*, to acknowledge *Him* as "the Way, the Truth, and the Life"—means that we opt for an escape from slavery to moral error.

The visible sign of Baptism, water immersion, symbolizes death to the power of sin and resurrection to a new life purified in freedom. As we advance toward that more mature degree of integrated spirituality in which salvation sign and living experience meld together, the familiar baptismal action should reveal itself to us in a new light. For over and above the momentary ceremonial immersion of the body, it signifies the life-long plunge of the human spirit into the mystery of Christ.

On December 4, 1963 the first document of the Second Vatican Council was promulgated. It is more than coincidental that that keynote-sounding declaration was the *Constitution on The Sacred Liturgy*. Updated theological understanding and liturgical exercise of the sacraments have been at the forefront of the renewal movement. Ranking high among the more important advances has been the rekindled emphasis on Penance as that "sacrament of initiation" intimately linked to the goal and graces of Baptism.

Until more recent years Penance appeared stigmatized, particularly in the catechesis young Catholics were receiving, as something of a "second rate" sacrament, a purgation rite functioning as little more than a soul-cleansing prelude to the reception of Holy Eucharist.

The more recent encouragement given by bishops and religious educators to defer first reception of Penance until after a child's First Holy Communion has been a particularly welcome development, and a healthy one for Christian sacramental life. For separation of these two vital sacraments permits a more intensified catechesis, and hence a firmer appreciation in the child's mind for each. Especially in regard to Penance, its deferred reception allows time for a more mature understanding of reconciliation to grow within the young person, and greater opportunity is given teachers to foster the notion of Penance as the Christ-centered source of forgiveness for deviations from our Baptismal commitment.

Some confusion arose as to the continued permissibility of First Communion reception before Penance for children when the Sacred Congregation for the Clergy issued a letter to the American hierarchy in March 1973. The Congregation declared that the "experimental practice" of deferring Penance until after First Communion was to be ended. This Vatican letter declared itself based on the norms prescribed in Pope Pius X's encyclical *Quam Singulari* released in 1910.

A number of American bishops were distressed by this unanticipated decree. Bishop Charles Buswell of Pueblo, Colorado echoed the sentiments of many bishops when he stated:

> "I am convinced that the reception of first communion before first confession is based on good theology, is rooted on solid findings of the behavioral sciences and is excellent pastoral practice. . . I foresee most of the leading religious educators of our country and not a few bishops expressing respectful dissent to this 'declaration' even as I do."

There was strong sentiment that the Congregation's letter failed to reflect either adequate consultation with the

United States' hierarchy or sufficient pastoral sensitivity to a development widely regarded as promising.

At the November 1973 annual meeting of the American bishops in Washington Archbishop William Borders, heading the Committee on Education of the National Conference of Catholic Bishops, issued a report on the understanding and implementation of the Congregation's decree that was most favorably received by the bishops. Briefly, Archbishop Borders pointed out that *Quam Singulari* was an important document intended to end the abusive practice of *denying* Penance to youngsters until the then-common age for First Communion—about 12 or 13 years old. It ordered the "age of discretion" reduced to approximately seven years of age. It did *not* state that there was an obligation to confess before receiving First Communion.

Referring to the principles outlined in the recent *General Catechetical Directory* from Rome, Archbishop Borders' report stressed the necessity of parental involvement in the sacramental preparation of the child, and the obligation of parents, pastor, and religious educator of the child to participate in determining the child's preparedness to receive the first sacraments. Care must be taken that no child is deprived of Penance or Holy Eucharist when deemed sufficiently ready. Also, catechesis on both Penance and Eucharist should be given before either is received.

It was the consensus of the American bishops that programs allowing Penance to be received after First Communion may be continued, and in fact the approved religious education guidelines of many dioceses encourage such programs while assuring that the preferences of parents and children in this matter are to be respected.

It is no less important for grown-ups to make confession an experience worthy of their maturity in Christ. Unhappily, many Catholics seem far more "childish" than "childlike" when approaching the encounter of forgiveness with their Father. Our motives for "hitting the box" sometimes amount to little more than "slate-cleaning" for some special churchy occasion, or at best "installment plan" payment entitling the premium-payer to x-number of Sundays at the communion rail.

On the other hand, if we conceive Penance as an opportunity to reconfirm our Baptismal union with Christ, and enter into it with a keen awareness of how dependent we are on its graces to combat the cancerous effects of the *primordial sin*, then we give evidence of advancement beyond the stage of spiritual babes.

What's more, like the athlete unstintingly devoted to sharpening his skills and expanding his endurance, we need the kind of spiritual conditioning for Penance that builds stamina in patience and in hope. For sometimes confessing frequently-recurring actual sins can become as frustrating as cutting garden weeds with a mower. While dispensed with for the present we know that our surface trimming has done nothing to attack their roots and prevent their return.

Further there is an insidious quality about our sinfulness. Our self-judgment can be perverted. Pride can persuade us to mask our weaknesses and hide even from ourselves. Great as they were, David, Solomon, and other Old Testament notables fell from favor, victimized by misplaced confidence in their righteousness before God. Wisely does the Psalmist cry, "Cleanse me of my unknown faults!" (Ps 19:13).

Not everyone who says "Lord, Lord!" will enter the Kingdom of heaven. Jesus does not want his followers intimidated by sin, but he does want them to appreciate that sin consists in more than violations of the old Law, and that it challenges man on every level of his existence. Where prayer is absent sin can corrode belief. Where charity is withheld hostility germinates. Without the "flesh" of good works, faith wastes like dry bones. Where old men despair of their visions and young men abandon hope-filled dreams, the sterile deceptions of illusion and ideology are bound to rush toward the vacuum.

Key passages in St. John's Gospel (cf. 15:18-25; 17:13-26) contrast "the world"—the kingdom of darkness—to the realm of salvation—life in the light of Christ. In his great priestly prayer Jesus calls upon his Father asking not that his disciples be taken *from* the world but that they might be "consecrated in truth" to identify and resist its errors (17:15-17). Likewise St. Paul pleads for recognition of sin as a full-blown cosmic reality. His warning is gravely direct:

> Our battle is not against human forces but against the principalities and powers, the rulers of this world of darkness... (Ep 6:12)

In other words the petty skirmishes we conduct against the "grocery list" of minor offenses we admit to in daily life can obscure our need to mobilize against the well-camouflaged sources of the enemy's real strength. The vapid business-as-usual norms and self-serving conventions, the cultural shibboleths and class prejudices, the myths of power, status or materialism, the subservience to passion, the general disregard for the dignity of self and others as children of God—these are among the true root bases of man's corruption, and they lead inexorably to the death of his spirit.

Chapter V

Christian Survival:
The Believer in the Unreconciled World

Seek first his kingship over you, his way of holiness, and all these things will be given you besides.
(Mt 6:33)

Christian faith sees man's moral situation as a part of the mystery of his existence; hopeful, yet delicate and complex. We are all victims of original sin, yet our redemption has been won. We cannot escape the effects of evil yet we remain free to choose the good. We are powerless over the past but may be masters of our future. With St. Paul (cf. Rm 7:13-24) we know the feeling of being at war with our members; flesh vs. spirit with no time-outs and no holds barred. We are at once children of darkness and of light; one with that universe that continues to groan through the struggle of sin and grace.

Moral tension is as real and unavoidable as any physical or emotional stresses that life invariably sends our way. Indeed societies and cultures are as much subject to moral anxiety as are individuals. Some of history's more intriguing chapters have been written around man's persistent efforts to cope with moral dilemmas.

Old Testament Israel, for instance, seized upon the Mosaic Law and wrapped itself around norms of conduct that it proclaimed as God-Authored, and thus definitive. Virtually all issues could be referred to the Law as the ultimate arbiter of behavior. Comparatively little in the way of judgmental decision-making was left to the individual conscience.

By contrast the modern existentialists have rushed to an opposite pole. Their banner is extreme cynicism. The universe is run amok. Neither absolute norms nor powers to enforce them exist. Reality is in fact absurdity, they declare, and man—in philosopher Jean-Paul Sartre's words—merely a "futile passion."

Marxism with its theory of dialectic (drawing heavily upon Hegel who in turn drew heavily on the classical school of Heraclitus) stakes out a middle ground. First, invalidate the obsolete moral concepts of good and evil. Man, grasping the helm of history, need look only to the beacons of utility and pragmatism. Recognize and respect the inevitability of change, the Marxist says. Permit it, even cultivate it, but above all *control* it with the Archimedean lever of economic class struggle.

What does Christianity tell us of man's condition? In contrast to the atheist existentialist the Christian affirms a God-centeredness to all creation. At the same time he concurs with St. Paul that such bulwarks of tradition as the Mosaic Law must not foreclose the action of God's Spirit in history. To those (such as the Marxists) who propose ideological formulas for governing man's behavior and regulating his destiny Christian wisdom responds by saying that to possess eternal Truth is not necessarily to have "all the answers."

Christianity sees the Church of Jesus Christ called to a special mission in the world. Listening with the ears and speaking with the voice of Christ, the Church is responsible for guiding God's People by the light of the Gospel. It cannot and must not pretend to possess pre-packaged instant solutions to any imaginable set of moral circumstances. The course of man's salvation cannot be computer-programmed. Man's *faith*, the Church teaches, does not reside in the Law, nor in ideology, nor in his own devices, but in the Way of Christ as it leads through the trial of the Cross to the glory of the Resurrection.

Something of the dynamism of this Way is captured in a cinematic technique used by director Pier Paolo Pasolini in his acclaimed film *Gospel According to St. Matthew.* A good deal of the action and dialogue occurs while Jesus and his disciples are in motion. In fact, Jesus' followers (and the movie's audience) must often strain to match his pace and catch his words as he strides—literally as well as symbolically —toward the Holy City, Calvary, and beyond.

Such a technique is faithful to the Gospel portrayal of Christ's all-consuming drive for his Father's Kingdom. He refuses compromise with the morally self-indulgent, even when his single-mindedness and religious purity earn him powerful enemies among the Pharisees and Sadducees. Jesus shows his exasperation with the casuistic quibbling of these professional religionists. He is appalled by the facile manner in which they interpret *God's* work as bound up on dietary rules, Sabbath regulations, and outright sophistry (cf. Mt 22:23-33). Their high threshold of tolerance for exploitation of the poor marks them as targets for the strongest words of condemnation to be found in the New Testament.

As compassionate as he is toward the sinner seeking forgiveness, Jesus bridles at any hint from his followers that popular acceptance might come easier should he temper the demands of his call to "perfection." With God, he says flatly, *all* things are possible. Jesus will not allow his Father to be mocked by moral values or religious priorities ordered to anything less than God's own image.

Jesus is not in the world to condemn or to endorse it as it is, but to revolutionize it. He is unafraid of confrontation and not bothered by controversy. In the tradition of the prophets he upsets the pseudo-peace between God and man that shelters the irresponsible behind vacuous pieties and perfunctory worship. It is this passion for the genuine "things of God" that flares as Jesus expels the buyers and sellers from the Temple on the occasion of his triumphal entry into Jerusalem. In that episode there is a sign as well as a deed. For Jesus is indignant at more than the conduct of worldly commerce on ground strictly dedicated to the worship of God. He is most outraged at the comparison physically established between the market place and the Sanctuary as the convenient, business-as-usual bartering place between God and man.

There is a divine recklessness about the Christ. His is not the close-to-the-vest, conservative-investment-for-secure-return ethic of the trade mart. He saves his earthiest utterance for the "lukewarm"; for those who adopt as their motto "moderation in all things—including virtue."

The Old Testament bears witness to the outrage of the Prophets at the same brand of religious adulteration Jesus finds at the gates of the Temple. Such scandals long predated Jesus' time and down through the history of Christianity they have wounded the body of believers in just about every age. As the Master warned in fiery language, the pagans who admitted no connection between "cult and code"—that is, the worship of the gods and the practice of morality—were far worthier in the Father's eyes than the Children of both Old and New Covenants who nodded assent to Revealed Truth, then proceeded to prostitute it.

> Mark what I say! Many will come from the east and the west and will find a place at the banquet in the kingdom of God with Abraham, Isaac, and Jacob, while the natural heirs of the kingdom will be driven out into the dark. Wailing will be heard there, and the grinding of teeth. (Mt 8:11-12)

Be doers of the word and not hearers only! Paul emphasized repeatedly that true faith was to be found only where Christian belief and practice were integrated. Where the two failed to mesh or fell victim to perversion there could be no genuine reconciliation in Christ. In our own time and culture—rather heavily-seasoned with what some have labeled "American civil religion"—we have recently been taught a lesson on how insipid the "salt" of religion can become when it loses the flavor of genuine Scriptural faith.

The tragedy of Watergate saw the fall-in-disgrace of an administration which passed up few opportunities to flaunt its public piety and endearment to religious values. As we now know, we passed through a period of hardcore political skulduggery in which some of this nation's highest officials were found to have countenanced break-ins, payoffs, harassment of political "enemies," illegal surveillance of American citizens, and widely-assorted varieties of justice obstruction to "cover up" all that had gone before. Conversely during this same period White House "prayer breakfasts" and regular Sunday services in the Executive mansion were being conducted on a scale never witnessed before. While war-protesting clergy were being ignored (or arrested) and civil rights champions of the stature of Rev. Theodore Hesburgh were being unseated from presidential commissions, "positive thinking" religious leaders such as Rev. Billy Graham and Dr. Norman Vincent Peale found themselves warmly received by White House congregations.**

When the state finds it expedient to utilize religion in its political propaganda machinery, and when the church finds

---

** This author admits to believing that theology and wit were both admirably served by the remark attributed to Adlai Stevenson when asked to comment on promoters of the "gospel of reassurance." Pointing to his copy of the Epistles Stevenson declared: "I find Paul appealing, and Peale appalling!"

it more appealing to make *profits* rather than produce *prophets,* the sacred trust of the faith is deeply jeopardized. Few redeeming social articles can be extracted from the tar-pit of Watergate, but there were men of conviction who prevailed over its evils, and stories which emerged that lend relevant setting to timeless moral lessons.

One especially suited to our present concern with "Christian survival" involves convicted Watergate defendant Jeb Magruder. Befriended while a student at Yale by chaplain William Sloan Coffin, the young man often sought Coffin's advice. On one occasion the chaplain offered him an observation which—in light of the scandal Magruder involved himself in—must have seemed sadly prescient. "Jeb," Coffin remarked, "you're a nice guy—but you're not yet a moral man. You'd better start standing for something, or you're liable to fall for anything."

Give all that you have and come, follow me! Leave the dead to bury the dead! See the birds of the air and the lilies of the field! Put hand to plow and don't look back! Jesus wants no stony institutional monument marking his moment in history. Rather he bleeds for the living love-sign memorial of those who do as he has done with his words burning in their hearts.

The term "radical" bears a host of unsavory connotations for many in our middle-class majority society. Depending on the viewpoint of the commentator, it can be used to brand anyone from a maniacal incendiary to someone we may dislike on the specious grounds that they seem "to go too far too fast." Polemical rhetoric has obscured the fact that the word means simply something *basic* or *prior to all else.* Still, for those with enough honesty and objectivity—those with "ears to hear" what the Gospels really say—Jesus reveals himself as the model "radical." For he speaks to the most fundamental concerns of man: life, future, and happiness.

By his words and his actions Jesus announces the coming of God's Reign; a new, lasting age in which human ("worldly") measures of success or failure are supplanted by God's. What really matters, Jesus teaches, is not whether we have met our personal—or society's imposed—standards of performance, but the conscientiousness with which we have been devoted to ". . . even these, the least of my brethren." There is more at stake here than sentimental humanism. Jesus insists that his followers be consumed, even as he is, with the desperate priority of living in God's love. That transcends all else. We may doubt, we may fail, we may sin. Yet nothing we do is beyond God's healing forgiveness so long as our style of living shows us *striving sincerely* toward reconciliation; reunion with ourselves, with others, with God our Father.

This thrust, this basic propulsion in our lives has been labeled by some contemporary theologians as our "fundamental option" or choice. It may be toward God or away from him. Though not always conscious of it, most practical decisions we make in regard to ourselves and others confirm or negate the option we have posted.

This "fundamental option" defies analysis in quantitative terms. No rapid calculation of actual sins committed or sacraments recently received can measure the strength of our choice. Free will always permits the alteration or reversal of our option, while God's judgment alone weighs the balance of our subjective "disposition" or ultimate capacity for responsibility in our moral actions. A simple lapse in virtue, for instance, need not alter our fundamental orientation toward the good; no more than fleeting praiseworthy gestures need indicate substantial change from a persistent refusal to live in God's grace.

Christians who live with motivation for thrusting forward into the life Christ offers can truly *enjoy* the sacramental occasions available to them. For in the "sacraments of initiation" (Baptism, Penance, Confirmation) we are given to understand that we are renewed in strength to live with the moral "gusto" and boldness characteristic of Jesus himself. Having been deputized to radical responsibilities by our Baptismal commitment, we are provided repeated opportunities to give religious expression to "the victory over sin and death" we share by our oneness with Christ.

Unfortunately, so many who "attend" the sacraments seem oblivious to any such thing. Large numbers of Catholics have "given up" on Penance altogether, and far too many who *do* come to confession act out their roles in it with a kind of enervated resignation. They envision themselves much like Sisyphus in the Greek myth—doomed to reach the crest of the hill (their act of confession) only to be rolled back to the valley again by the boulder-like weight of their inevitably recurring sins. For these unhappy souls Penance holds no opening for a promising future. It seems, rather, like a modest timberline beyond which survival is impossible and from which there is only downward retreat.

This attitude is especially distressing since it shows that the penitent considers himself undergoing a surrealistic appeasement rite, paying court to a capricious deity. In other words, confession becomes so misconstrued as to seem more for *God's* benefit than the sinner's!

Penance *should be* a full-bodied celebration of Hope. A healthy sense of elitism—a conviction that in God's grace we are called as a "chosen race, royal priesthood, and holy nation"—should stimulate our approach to the sacrament. So, while acknowledging our sinful failings, we remain mindful that we do that precisely because God has called us from the path of death to the way of Life, and therefore he expects us to lead others by our example. Because we are eager to be of greater service to the Kingdom in the future, we take the time and care to expose and examine our errors of the past.

A "sense of sin" that is informed by an appreciation of God's fundamental call for reconciliation can help us avoid the obstacles to religious development raised by the discredited "automatic car wash" school of spirituality. Confessors are all too familiar with the misguided attitudes of those who approach Penance handicapped by the exaggerated impersonalism of our computerized age. Just drive in, deposit the proper change in the meter, push the correct buttons, and sail through the churning brushes to emerge dry and spotless at the other end. Not only does this attitude betray a faulty, mechanical concept of sacramental grace, but it reveals something of the inordinate religious individualism prevalent in our day as well.

Perhaps because of the strong "laissez-faire" ethic that prevails in our culture, it is not uncommon to find those who feel that the business(!) of saving one's soul really amounts to an entrepreneurial venture. They see spiritual life as essentially an exercise in free enterprise; the religious "capitalist" investing moderately in virtue with hopes of realizing a whopping eternal reward. God, in such a view, takes on the appearance of an irascible Accountant—dyspeptic about man to begin with and eager to assess debits against our ledgers for the sins we commit.

Where virtue becomes a negotiable commodity to be traded off against the liability of our faults, moral living assumes a "work ethic" character. Today I'll "work on" humility . . . tomorrow I'll "work on" purity, etc. Consequently the concept of morality degenerates to a narrow-minded, rigorously individualistic level. Instead of setting an outbound course showing concern for others and happily welcoming opportunities to be available to their needs, we may find ourselves becoming progressively more self-conscious and self-serving in our obsession with "playing by the rules" and "avoiding occasions of sin." Sadly, many penitents indicate that their idea of living in the state of grace begins and ends as a "Jesus and me" tete-a-tete. They lack any real notion of sin as estrangement; rupture pleading for reconciliation with God *in* Person and through others *as* persons.

To some extent our past catechetical preoccupation with the self-directed concern for strategies helping me to "save my soul" may well have been at the expense of Christ's direct challenge to *lose our lives.* Jesus' exact words in this regard are worth pondering:

> If a man wishes to come after me, he must deny his very self, take up his cross, and begin to follow in my footsteps. Whoever would save his life will lose it, but whoever loses his life for my sake will find it. (Mt 16:24-25)

The glory of God, wrote St. Irenaeus of Antioch, is man fully alive. And "life to the full" begins as we pass with Christ through fear, through our old selves, through sin, and ultimately through death itself to freedom as God's homecoming children. There is no more radical a journey than the Way of the Cross-bearing Christ. The length and terrain of that journey will be unique for each of us since God's Spirit calls us personally to it. Yet our final destination is the same.

It is highly important that we see Christian life as an active, passionate commitment to receive God's Reign as it comes. It is hardly enough to flaunt those externals of our Catholic discipline (days of abstinence, regular Sunday Mass attendance, Easter duty, etc.) as the most prominent examples of what truly distinguishes us from the "world." Despite its internal problems, institutional religion today remains too easily identified in the public mind with the "establishment" norms of social acceptability, administrative efficiency, and financial affluence. We need, therefore, a particularly strong, refreshing witness among Christian communities to the "otherness" of God's Kingdom. We need the kind of witness displayed by Jesus himself and his apostles.

We *should* proclaim our distinctiveness. Yet we must keep in mind that what we bear as our sign is the sacrificial offering we make of ourselves through, with, and in Christ. Not by any assumed superiority as enrolled members in the "one, true Church" are we different from the non-believer, but by virtue of our efforts in moral practice, liturgical-sacramental celebration, creed and prayer to lead the genuinely *spiritual* life.

Nor may we be satisfied to remain at that stage of spiritual pre-puberty where "giving up" substitutes for *giving away*. To those who express anxiety that the Catholic Church is becoming less distinguishable from other denominations or is in some way softening its position on the necessity of *sacrifice*, we must give firm, and if necessary corrective responses.

While a practiced self-discipline is imperative for the devoted disciple of Christ, it must always function as a means of marshalling our energies for God's work among our neighbors, never as a conscience-quieting or guilt-assuaging device serving as an end in itself. The statements of the recent popes when modifying regulations or disciplines have emphasized that Church law should always act as a springboard to apostolic activity, not as a Pharisaic alternative to it. As early as St. Paul's writings we have evidence of the Church affirming that creative action for others on Christ's behalf is the most stirring of all challenges and the complete fulfillment of all God's Law.

Chapter VI

Penance: Sacrament for Getting in Touch

In his allocution announcing the Holy Year of 1975,
Pope Paul explained that its purpose was to stir more attention in the Church to the alienated condition of modern man.
Like those astronauts who found technological accomplishment an unsatisfactory substitute for humanitarian outreach
to the needy, as well as a meager diet for their personal spiritual growth, many who assumed that the sheer complexity of
modern life would sustain their enthusiasm for it are growing
fearful and disillusioned. Plato's ancient dictum about the
unexamined, the unreconciled, life being not worth living
seems to thrive with age.

In his call for renewal in the Church's mission of reconciliation Pope Paul spoke on behalf of those "no longer sufficiently in touch . . ." with the real world of spirit and flesh.
Many suffer self-estrangement from neglect of intellectual
or emotional development, from chronic indifference to
moral values, and from outright abuse of their own interior
lives. Being so "out of touch" with themselves has left many
oblivious to their roles and responsibilities in the larger communities of man outside themselves. The restless craving for
novelty, the continuous demand for diversionary entertain-
ments, the diminishing "sense of the sacred" pointing toward

the transcendent, the general inability to cope with *truth*—these and other symptoms suggest a real but unspoken fear too chilling for all but the bravest to face. Could it be that the frenzied excitement attending man's most materially prolific era—our Nuclear Age—amounts to no more than that instant when a candle flame flares with its most brilliant incandescence—the moment before it burns itself out?

Since the Second Vatican Council a movement has been underway in the Church to bring a greater measure of the healing, reconciling powers of the Sacrament of Penance to the aid of believers striving to cope with the realities of late 20th Century life. The revitalization of Penance has become a leading priority of numerous apostolates. Educators formulating primary and grammar school curricula in religion stress the importance of introducing Penance to younger children as a joyful opportunity to accept God's love and to plan better ways of sharing it with others. We counsel our adolescents to seek in confession a comforting sign of God's understanding and encouragement in the struggles for adjustment and development characteristic of the teenage years. On the parish and group level our bishops have endorsed the enhancement of the Sacrament's liturgical expression through seasonal penitential services and communal celebrations of Penance. The *Order of Penance*, an important document issued in February 1974 by the Church's Congregation for Divine Worship, cites the necessity of building the social spirit of reconciliation through communal penitential liturgies, and de-mechanizing individual confession through a more personalized exchange of prayer, Scripture-Reading, and full imposition of hands at absolution.

Penance offers the opportunity to "keep in touch" with what is really going on inside and outside ourselves. However, as with any "communications network" power failures or short circuits can impede or cut off altogether the vital flow of transmission. Myth and misconceptions about Penance have damaged its image. As a result some believe it to be unreasonably threatening, others dismiss it as so innocuous as to be time-wasting. The Sacrament's social dimension has too often been ignored while its interior effects, one tends to feel, have not been sufficiently understood even by many regular confession-goers. In general, worries about what we should be "telling" in confession have usurped the more basic issue of what the Sacrament can *tell us* about ourselves.

GUILT VS. SHAME

It would come as a shock to many penitents to learn that the object of the Sacrament of Penance is *not* to humiliate them. Humiliation, debasement, embarrassment—these are all synonyms for *shame;* and shame—clinically defined as that sense of remorse resulting purely from the ". . . exposure of peculiarly sensitive, intimate, vulnerable aspects of the self . . ."** is not what Penance is all about.

Shame denotes an injured sense of self-esteem that comes either from getting *caught* in the act of violating some law or norm, or in being forced to admit publicly such violation. Notice that we need have no internalized value for the norm we violate in order for the sense of shame to be stimulated.

Take for instance the case of a man stopped and ticketed by a police officer for jaywalking. Perhaps he has for years crossed in the middle of a particular block with either no adversion to the fact of violating a traffic law at all, or at least no internal uneasiness that what he does should cause him to feel remorse. Only when apprehended by the police-

---

** *On Shame and The Search for Identity,* by Helen M. Lynd, p. 27.

man does the jaywalker feel any such sensation, and *that* only because of the social stigma he knows he will incur as a lawbreaker.

As a matter of course there is a normal amount of ego-deflation we experience in the recounting of our sins to a confessor. We are facing up to our failure to meet the Christian standards of perfection. Yet feeling ashamed when confessing violation of what we believe (or what we have been told to believe) are God-given norms, says nothing about our true interior disposition toward those norms.

For example the penitent who confesses he "swore about 100 times" or was "angry about 50 times" virtually every time he comes to confession may well feel some sense of embarrassment at the necessity of mentioning the frequency of his offenses. Still, he gives the impression that he more or less accepts the presence of this behavior pattern as habitual, has no real intention of fighting it nor any strategy for overcoming it, and considers the humiliation of confessing it an act of purgation that of itself earns him justification before God.

Curiously, the presence of shame in the act of confessing can evoke two contrasting reactions. For some the shame that is assumed to attend the confessing of sins to a priest acts as the stumbling block that keeps them from the Sacrament—or in some cases from the Catholic Church entirely. Others, though, see the Church's mandate for auricular confession as a clever and necessary shame-stimulating device. As a disciplinary measure, they feel, it provides the kind of "negative reinforcement" that spurs improvement in future behavior.

Neither attitude is a sound one. For the sacramental encounter with Christ in Penance is not based on the self-pitying sense of shame. Its power is not derived from exploiting the emotional inferiority that results from failure to meet externally-imposed norms.

Penance is our sacramental opportunity to acknowledge direct responsibility for ignoring or rejecting God's call. That responsibility for sin we call *guilt.*

Where shame characterizes our depression at failing to meet standards imposed from without, guilt supposes the willful violation of norms we have internalized; that is, accepted as inherently good and declared to be our own.

An ethic constructed around shame relies on feelings of inadequacy. It feeds on self-abnegation and may lead one ultimately to despair. The shame-ethic is fundamentally pessimistic about the ability of man to live morally and thus depends heavily on the threat of disciplinary sanctions to keep him within the bounds of law. Luther and the Reformers tended to extol shame as a healthy sign of the appropriate self-rejection man should feel as a result of his inherent corruption.

Jesus, on the other hand, called forth repentance from sinners by appealing to the real potential he saw within them for nobility and goodness. The woman taken in adultery is uplifted in spirit and motivated to purity by the action Jesus takes to dramatize that none of her accusers are less in need of God's mercy than she. Zacchaeus proclaims a drastic change of heart for the better as Jesus' request for his hospitality frees him from the personal insecurity he had previously sought to resolve through domineering exploitation of others.

In each of these cases sin is neither ignored nor rationalized away. It is unmasked for what it is—a self- and other-destructive weakness. Guilt presents to the sinner both an elicited sense of responsibility for the moral failure in the first place, *and* the challenge to rectify the evil done. Guilt urges upon us both the weight and the power of responsibility. In contrast to the "cop-out" of shame, guilt impels us to do away with the evil, not with ourselves.

Early Freudian analysis settled on guilt as the source of man's enslavement to the past. It saw in guilt the shackles binding man's psyche within the confines of self-recriminating doubts and anxiety. Freedom from such constraint through psychoanalysis was held out as a utopian hope for those tortured by the inner conflicts. More recent schools of analysis and therapy have shown deeper understanding of the nature of moral guilt, rightfully distinguishing it from neurotic self-depredation. At the same time Catholic moral theology has incorporated some valuable insights gained from the life and social sciences regarding emotional illness, psychopathology, and the various pre-conscious and sociological factors influencing personality development. Psychology and Christian ethics have much to say to each other, but for our immediate purposes it is sufficient to affirm that traditional Catholic teaching sees legitimate guilt not as the representation of man's basic inner weakness, but in fact the sign of his facultative health. For despite our susceptibility to psychological stress and even disorientation, the acknowledgment of guilt in the mentally stable personality indicates a sound moral perceptiveness rather than a psychic pathology.

Unlike shame which involves distress at the mere uncovery of sub-standard performance, guilt functions as our persistent moral prosecutor. It forces us to admit that our free will has made a choice against the good. It also reminds us of our complicity in any harmful secondary or indirect effects that may spread from our original action. The first stirrings of guilt serve notice that the time has come for repentance and amendment.

The way we examine our conscience before confession says much about how maturely and sincerely we handle our sense of guilt. Shame at violation of norms is relatively easy to conjure up. We shrug and (at least implicitly) reason:

"Well, I've 'played the game' against temptation with what I reckon as a 50-50 chance of success (except in those moral areas where the 'handicap' of my habitual failures has lessened the percentage of my chances for holiness), and all told I've come out on the 'losing end' x number of times in y moral categories."

There is an air of defeatism in this type of reasoning, and that kind of sluggish resignation is too pervasive in the popular notion of Penance. Witness the perplexity of many Catholics over the idea of "celebrating" the Sacrament of Penance. Celebration suggests a rejoicing at victory over sin or exaltation at reconciliation in the forgiving Lord. For many, though, going to confession amounts only to indulging a moral inferiority complex. We have no doubt that God's power to forgive is present in the sacrament, but to believe that graces promoting future improvement are there also strains our credulity. Regrettably, for those resigned to convictions of perpetual moral inferiority Penance offers no real *healing* of moral wounds; only the periodic draining of chronically-infected and permanently open sores.

The potential benefits of Penance are lost on those who fail to find in it much more than a ritual recounting of innocence lost. But for those who begin preparation for confession with a prayerful, Scripture-centered examination of conscience, the pitfalls of a morbid, shame-centered preoccupation with spiritual bankruptcy can be avoided. First we should remind ourselves that Penance gives here-and-now extension to God's saving work begun within us at Baptism. Penance leads us once more toward total rebirth in the New Man for Christ. And to be spiritually reborn means something far greater than being purgatively "recycled." It is on this promising note that Penance starts to build its theme of Joy and Hope.

Jesus' parable of the talents (Mt 25:14-30) offers a

particularly meaty confessional meditation. It is sobering fare inasmuch as the master in the story rejects the servant who failed to use and multiply even the single talent he was given. Yet it is also reassuring since Jesus draws out of it the lesson that none of God's children enters the world as a spiritual orphan. In the apportionment of His blessings, our Father imparts to each of us the most precious of His "talents"—the "inexpressible gift" as St. Paul has it (2 Cor 9:15) of life in God's love.

It is then from a position of strength rather than weakness before the world that the person of faith deals with it. The Sacrament of Penance invites us to come before the Father expressing genuine sorrow born of our guilt for ignoring or abusing His goodness. He, in turn, accepts our contrition even if imperfect and motivated by fear of punishment. Yet to the extent we allow Him to do so, God's Holy Spirit evokes from us recognition that true repentance should begin from a sense of remorse at responsibility failed rather than merely shame and fear at law transgressed.

The forgiveness eagerly granted by our Father should of itself supply one of the strongest motives for a vigorous spirit of amendment. For He Himself has given us the most inspiring example of the shape our renewed moral efforts ought to take. In the lyrics of Oscar Hammerstein:

> Love in your heart wasn't put there to stay;
> Love is not love till you give it away!

TURN, TURN, TURN

> The human race has passed from a rather static concept of reality to a more dynamic, revolutionary one. In consequence there has arisen a new series of problems, a series as important as can be, calling for new efforts of analysis and synthesis.
>
> —Decree on The Church in the Modern World

> To live is to change,
> And to be perfect is to have changed often.
>
> —John Henry Newman

Opening his public ministry Jesus began his proclamation of God's Reign coming with a call for repentance. Aligning himself with John the Baptist and with the prophets of Old Testament tradition, he summoned his hearers to a new level of spiritual existence initiated by a radical change of heart. He called for renunciation of sin as a purifying preliminary to reception of a whole new awareness of God's activity in the world and of our place in His plans.

The modern, youth-bred revival of interest in the person of Jesus (cf. the faddish "Jesus Movement"; the pop-rock musicals *Jesus Christ Superstar, Godspell,* etc.) indicates among other things that even in our highly turbulent era the mere fact of rapid turnover in the conventions and accouterments of society leaves those who seek real *change,* of the kind Jesus preached, unfulfilled.

Authentic change does not mean jettisoning periodically everything that has been good in our past or in the Church's. It does mean that we enter constantly into the prayerful search for wisdom and prudence. These virtues help us discern whether the vehicles and structures designed to aid the advance of the Kingdom in one age or set of historical circumstances will be serviceable or obsolete in the next.

American folksinger Pete Seeger composed a musical adaptation of Ecclesiastes 3:1-8, that poetic Old Testament litany of life's pendulum swings ("A time to weep, and a time to laugh; a time to mourn, and a time to dance...", etc.) which he entitled *Turn, Turn, Turn.* "For everything there is a season," the refrain echoes, "and a time for every purpose under heaven."

The Sacrament of Penance calls our attention to the numerous *turns,* the constant gear-shifting adjustments to be made in our living patterns if we are to keep pace with the Holy Spirit's manifestation in what Pope John XXIII and the Vatican Council Fathers alluded to as the changing "signs of the times."**

As orthodox Christians we do not pretend to harbor occult apocalyptic blueprints for the coming of God's Kingdom. Only the religiously fanatic make such claims. Rather we seek to be open, in daily life situations, to new opportunities for extending God's good work well-begun in us ever further into the family of man.

There is a "ripple effect" to our every moral action, good and bad. Penance bids us see which boats are being rocked gently and which are threatening to capsize as our pebbles are tossed in the pool. To do this we must make certain that our examination of conscience before confession does not stop with the simple identification of our failures. Nor can we let the casual mental note to "try to avoid" some particular evil the next time it comes around suffice for genuine purpose of amendment. There must be both a positive strategy and a clear futurity on which to anchor repentance— *authentic change*—in our lives.

We should, for instance, cultivate what we described earlier as the outward-bound dimension to our Christian character. This means we start building our apostolic efforts on the foundation of the particular environment in which we find ourselves. Who and where we are, what we do, whom we know, what special talents or abilities God has blessed us with, which crosses we are asked to bear—all of these influence the direction in which the Spirit is blowing for us.

If I am newly married, for example, am I attentive to all the grace possibilities of the Spring-fresh romantic love

---

**See *Pacem in Terris* and Vatican II's *Decree on The Church in The Modern World*, paragraph #4.

I am now sharing with my partner? Do I permit it to blossom in the kind of joyful spirit that may brighten the day of those I work with or meet? If I am older in married years has the wisdom born of sacrifice sensitized me to the needs of those I see struggling with marital problems? At home am I replenishing my family with the creative energy sparked for me by the loving support of my spouse? As a housewife has natural concern for my family's welfare led to a broadened involvement in the similar interests of neighborhood and community? As an adolescent is my growing passion for self-identity teaching me greater respect for the rights and dignity of others? If happy am I sharing my happiness? If saddened am I learning more of compassion? If troubled or fearful am I deepening in appreciation for the urgency in human need? What sort of person do I *need to become?*

A multitude of such personally-applicable questions can erupt as we begin to see ourselves in confession not simply as passive receivers of absolution but as active communicators of reconciliation. The Sacrament of Penance was never intended as a means of instant restoration to a carefree, spiritually-pristine Garden of Eden. It provides rather for our reinvigorated return to that vineyard where, with Paul and Apollos, we can "plant and water" that God may give the growth.

CATHOLIC MEANS UNIVERSAL

> Action on behalf of justice and participation in the transformation of the world appear to us as a constitutive dimension of the preaching of the Gospel, or, in other words, of the Church's mission for the redemption of the human race and its liberation from every oppressive situation. . .
>
> Since men are members of the same human family they are indissolubly linked with one another in the

one destiny of the whole world, in the responsibility
for which they all share.
              —Decree *Justice in The World*
                  Synod of Bishops, 1971

The inward-turning aspect of Penance helps reveal who
we are right now. Searching yet estranged in many ways
from full union with God and others, we seek those frank
answers of ourselves that tell of where and how we have
failed to cooperate with God's grace.

The "outward-turning" stage of our Penance celebration
finds us charting that corrected course toward the Kingdom
that steers by the new breeze of the Holy Spirit in our lives.
Here the sacrament should guide us toward a *universalism*
in our moral vision.

Guilt is triggered by our failure to live up to acknowledged personal moral responsibilities. In addition the informed Christian conscience recognizes accountability both
for the presence of evil and the promotion of good far beyond the immediate range of our personal and interpersonal
affairs.

St. Paul confronts us with the related doctrines of original sin and the Body of Christ. In the former (cf. Rm 5:12ff)
Paul teaches that as we have all sinned in Adam so none of
us can escape the effects of primordial sin as they are dif-
fused throughout all creation. Nor may we disavow responsibility for the evil perpetrated by others whether far or near.
We who profess to live in the power of God's grace can never
plead total impotence before the threat of evil, however
massive its proportions or removed from us in time or space.
The Christian may never wash his hands of innocent blood.
Sacred Scripture does not equivocate about the Christian's
duty as his brother's keeper. Pastor Martin Niemoeller,
recalling his crisis of conscience during the early years of

Hitler's regime, speaks first hand of the nightmare man may create for himself by shirking this duty:

> In Germany, the Nazis first came for the Communists, and I didn't speak up because I was not a Communist. Then they came for the Jews, and I didn't speak up because I was not a Jew. Then they came for the trade unionists, and I didn't speak up because I wasn't a trade unionist. Then they came for the Catholics, and I was a Protestant, so I didn't speak up. Then they came for me . . . by that time there was no one to speak for anyone.

As members of the universal Body of Christ we must never forget that sin as well as grace has a communal reality. Societies, cultures, and institutions can breed and carry infectious evil as well as any individual. Indeed our failure to deal with the "corporate personality" of evil as it conducts itself through the channels of our social systems is among the most serious of our "sins of omission." Addressing his Archdiocesan clergy on July 2, 1972, Cardinal John Cody of Chicago observed:

> The priest must identify the sins of the community and, insofar as he can, lead his people from them. The tolerance of war is one such sin. Insensitivity to poverty at home and abroad is another. Indignity and injustice because of racial or religious differences are still further examples. All of these reside in the hearts of individuals, but they achieve their evil effects most tellingly in the activity or inactivity of communities.

The documents of Vatican II in reference to man's contemporary moral condition are especially harsh on the complacency afforded by "individualistic morality":

> Profound and rapid changes make it particularly urgent that no one, ignoring the trend of events or drugged by laziness, content himself with a merely individualistic morality. It grows increasingly true

that the obligations of justice and love are fulfilled
only if each person, contributing to the common good,
according to his own abilities and the needs of others,
also promotes and assists the public and private institutions dedicated to bettering the conditions of
human life.

Yet there are those who, while professing grand and
rather noble sentiments, nevertheless in reality live
always as if they cared nothing for the needs of society. (*Decree on The Church in The Modern World*,
paragraph 30.)

That our moral responsibilities are worldwide is not an
axiom of some "far out" speculative theology, but in fact is
an article of our faith. "Go, therefore, and make disciples of
all the nations" (Mt 28:19) Jesus tells his followers. Through
the 12th and 13th chapters of First Corinthians we find the
universalist vision of the Church's greatest missionary verbalized in terms of the *Body of Christ.* As members of that
One Body each of us is responsible to all other members
and to the One Lord for the upbuilding of the whole.

As an official, sacred *sign of Christ* present to us, particularly in his ministry of Healer and Reconciler of all mankind, the Sacrament of Penance is a prime source of revelation and teaching on the mystery of the Body of Christ.
Bowed down as we are by sin, Penance raises us up, and in
doing so it should afford us the advantage of a higher ground
from which our moral vision can range farther and wider
than ever. If we choose not to be instructed in the lessons
of universal reconciliation; if we continue to opt for buck-
passing, apathy, and perpetual hibernation within self-con-
structed shells of prejudice, then we admit our stubborn
unwillingness to pay the cost of discipleship in Christ. We
number ourselves then among those many called, yet found
unworthy to be chosen. We show that our real sentiments
lie with the philosophy of Lucy Van Pelt, worldly-wise mop-

pet of the *Peanuts* cartoon strip. "I love all mankind," Lucy declaims, "it's *people* I can't stand!"

God hardly expects us to rush full-tilt into every fray, or to fire off instant solutions to every world dilemma like trigger-happy Western gunslingers. The point is as Christians we must be willing to claim the world community as our own; its problems rate my attention, its sinfulness necessitates my sanctity, its holiness depends on my dedication. I sin by doing nothing when it is apparent that there is much to be done.

In concluding the address from which we quoted above, Chicago's Cardinal Cody offered his priests both a hope and a challenge:

> Look forward to the day when your people approach the Sacrament of Penance to confess as their own, sins which are now commonly assigned to the community. When you hear complacency about war, indifference to poverty, and participation in racism and bigotry mentioned in the confessional, you will know that the remission of sins in the fullest sense of these words has been dealt with faithfully and successfully.

Chapter VII

Penitential Conversion - The Gift of Empathy

"First of all," he said, "if you can learn a simple trick,
Scout, you'll get along a lot better with all kinds of
folks. You never really understand a person until you
consider things from his point of view—"
"Sir?"
"—until you climb into his skin and walk around in it."
—Atticus Finch
To Kill A Mockingbird

Before his dramatic conversion St. Paul was the epitome
of the religious "redneck." His was the equivalent of an
aristocratic education in rabbinical learning which held an
uncompromising faith in the exclusiveness of the Chosen
People as the recipients of God's favor. In fact, this steadfast
conviction so tempered Paul's zeal for religious purity that
he committed himself to stamping out the perversions of
those who—calling themselves "Christians"—dared suggest
that God had offered a new Way of salvation, available to
Jew and Gentile alike.

Precisely because Paul's religious convictions were so
deep on just this matter of limited divine election, his conversion to faith in the universal salvific power of Christ must
rank as one of the great reversals of all time. Since the traditions of our society are so steeped in pluralism we are accustomed to hearing brotherhood, equality, ethnic and religious
tolerance, etc., at least preached (if not always admitted in

practice) as "self-evident truths." However, for Paul, erst-
while rabbinic firebrand, to declare that "there are no more
distinctions between Jew and Greek, slave and free, male
and female, but all of you are one in Christ Jesus" (Gal 3:28)
was nothing less than an astounding recantation. He goes
on to justify his change of heart by asserting that this teaching was "unknown to men in former ages" (Ep 3:5), coming
only through revelation in the mystery of Christ.

Before encountering Christ on that fateful ride to
Damascus Paul believed that the Mosaic Law dictated the
rules for his ethical thought and behavior. With conversion,
agape—love for all in Christ—became his standard for moral
living. It is then with a special poignant intensity that Paul,
persecutor-turned-proselyte of Christianity, pleads with his
brethren "to live a life worthy of the calling you have received" (Ep 4:1). He appeals to his listeners not as blood-
heirs of an old covenant sealed by their adherence to the
Law, but as new, free persons sharing brotherhood with all
in Christ as adopted sons and daughters of their heavenly
Father. The Christian life, Paul teaches, consists in respond-
ing to God's call for reconciliation; for *oneness* in life with
the Source of all life:

> Make every effort to preserve the unity which has the
> Spirit as its origin and peace as its binding force.
> (Ep 4:3)

It is not difficult to feel morally superior to the unen-
lightened, intolerant Saul of Tarsus. Most of us raised from
birth as Christians have little conception of what it is to be
knocked (literally and figuratively) from a high horse of
religious wrongheadedness. Consequently neither is it easy
for us to comprehend the startlingly new relationship with
others as well as with God that Paul awoke to as the scales
fell from his eyes.

After all, we have been baptized and confirmed. We

have been raised in religious families and educated in our faith. We receive the sacraments regularly, live by the Ten Commandments, support the Church and obey its precepts. Surely if anyone *knows* what Christianity is all about; if anyone is less in need of the bone-rattling conversion experience Paul underwent, then it is you and I!

Or is it?

Conversion, as Paul's experience attests, involves considerably more than intellectual assent to articles of belief. Also it is not something that happens once for all time. In Christian tradition "conversion" is best explained by what the ancient Greeks referred to as *metanoia*—profound, ongoing transformation in life meaning and direction. It connotes an awakening to a dimension of God's life in our own previously undiscovered.

Thus conversion is not limited to those who adopt new religious beliefs, and it means more than a one-shot exchange of perfidy for piety. As *change of heart* conversion includes a yielding to the Gifts of the Holy Spirit, and in particular to that charism the spiritual fathers have labeled "fear of the Lord."

Commonly misunderstood as implying a shuddering terror at the power of God to punish, fear of the Lord really means a virtuous *respect for God's prerogatives*. We display it when we refuse to "grieve the Spirit" by the self-righteous brand of religious snobbery that dismisses the possibility that God may act through any but the "traditional" forms, institutions or persons He has used to reveal Himself in the past. Fear of the Lord calls on us to show a forward-looking openness of the heart. It means we test our faith constantly and carefully, making sure that it is not being "co-opted" by cultural fads, cabal-like devotions, or attachment to partisan or exclusivist religious cliques. Conversion summons us to Faith in God's Present, Hope in His Future, and Love in all.

For St. Paul conversion to Christianity came as the break of a new dawn, illuminating a religious horizon of much broader dimensions than he had ever suspected. Before experiencing Christ Paul peered from behind the vision-narrowing blinders of religious obstinacy. He believed that the children of Abraham, guided by the Law of Moses, were the only travelers on the road to salvation. The impact of his unanticipated meeting with the Risen Lord left Paul wide-eyed at the "length and breadth, the height and the depth" (Ep 3:18) of God's plan for reconciling all creation to Himself in Christ, the Lord and Brother of all men.

The new person in Christ, Paul preaches, is the *whole* person, the universal citizen of a Kingdom-bound world. Each of us is called by the Father through the Son ". . . to be holy and blameless in his sight, to be full of love" (Ep 1:4). Each is enjoined to ". . . acquire a fresh, spiritual way of thinking . . . (to) put on that new man created in God's image, whose justice and holiness are born of truth."

Paul sees the act of Redemption begun by Christ's "outpouring" or self-emptying; first into the condition of man through the Incarnation, and then into the Providence of God through surrender to the passion and death prelude to the Resurrection. As Paul starts to recount the trial and glory of the Self-sacrificing Christ in the "panegyric hymn" portion of Philippians, he urges believers to see themselves as imitators of the example Jesus sets:

> . . . make my joy complete by your unanimity, possessing the one love, united in spirit and ideals. Never act out of rivalry or conceit; rather, let all parties think humbly of others as superior to themselves, each of you looking to others' interests rather than your own. Your attitude must be that of Christ. (Ph 2:1-5)

Paul understands that as members of the One Body we commit ourselves to strong bonds with our neighbor. Much more is demanded than that we simply work together for the smooth, efficient functioning of society. Since it is in Christ that we have our member-ship, we participate in what He does; namely, healing and uniting each other in Him. Just as Christ represents the initiative of God stepping out of Godhood to "put on" man, so each of us must step out of ourselves and into the lives of others if we would truly "put on Christ" (cf. Col 3:9-11).

Related to the Sacrament of Penance, this means that our continuous conversion to a deeper knowledge of Christ leads us to a deepening sense of *spiritual empathy* for our neighbor.

Reformation theology brought into vogue the idea that Redemption was basically an act of divine *sympathy;* a result of God's "feeling sorry" for man's sinful plight. But the revealed entrance of God into the situation of man is not so much characterized by a "feeling *for*" as by a "feeling *with.*" God's Plan brought Him into the thick of man's predicament. In Christ God Himself identified with the human condition, became vulnerable to its powerlessness, felt its sufferings, and allowed Himself to be visited by its most appalling devastation. Under the weight of sin's full force against man, the Spirit of God in Jesus prevailed throughout his life. Taking on Death itself Christ revealed by His Resurrection that the life-of-God-in-man leads inexorably to glory. God refuses to permit His faithful ones to undergo corruption.

United as we are with the self-sacrificial outpouring of Christ, we bear responsibility as His followers not merely to preach or *acknowledge brotherhood,* but to *feel* and share it. We have a serious obligation to do more than voice platitudes about bridge-building and unity. The New Testament warns against being subjective or cattily selective about those to whom we reach out in charity. In particular the Letter of James, with its emphasis upon "true religion" revealed through good works, shows an unwavering "hard line" when it comes to the Christian's role in social concern:

> Do not try to combine faith in Jesus Christ, our glorified Lord, with the making of distinctions between classes of people . . . Take the case . . . of someone who has never done a single good act but claims that he has faith. Will that faith save him? If one of the brothers or one of the sisters is in need of clothes and has not enough food to live on, and one of you says to them, 'I wish you well; keep yourself warm and eat plenty,' without giving them these bare necessities of life, then what good is that? Faith is like that: if good works do not go with it, it is quite dead. (Jm 2:1, 14-17)

The old saw about being obliged "to love" while not being required "to like" has no place in the truly Christian ethic. While personality conflicts and other divisive factors may obstruct our compatibility with some, Christian behavior demands that we never remain satisfied with arranging relationships on a "permanent stalemate" basis. With prudence and good will as our guidelines we are required to maintain momentum toward reconciliation. The prayerfully strong, sensitive heart keeps probing for those openings that may allow us to grow closer to those from whom we have been separated.

As Jesus Himself remarked, loving only those we find it easy to love is unexceptional—"do not the pagans do as much?" (Mt 5:47). The challenge that makes us worthy of our Christian calling is to strip away as many layers of difference as may be necessary to reach the common center of likeness with another. Just as the contemporary ecumenical movement in religion strives (without whitewashing existing doctrinal differences) to build upon the mutual strengths, mission, and needs of all the churches, the grace of Christian empathy permits us to sink the roots of our faith ever deeper into that firm ground which Pope Paul refers to as "human solidarity":

> There can be no progress toward the complete development of man without the simultaneous development of all humanity in the spirit of solidarity. As we said in Bombay: 'Man must meet man, nation must meet nation, as brothers and sisters, as children of God. In this mutual understanding and friendship, in this sacred communion, we must also begin to work together to build the common future of the human race.' *On The Development of Peoples*, paragraph 43)

By its nature as a sign of God's desire to forgive and accept each of us equally and completely as His children, sacramental Penance makes a particularly strong appeal to our sense of solidarity. Take, for instance, the relation of penitential conversion to Jesus' observation "the poor you have always with you" (Jn 12:8). Those who are in material need, quite obviously subsisting at a much lower level than the living standard for their society, are readily identifiable as "poor." Yet how often are we reminded that material poverty is but *one way* of being poor? Aren't there many around us pitifully underprivileged largely because of their material wealth? What of those who have consistently deprived themselves of developing any but superficial material values? What of the literally millions in our land alone—products of ticky-tacky social conformity, the production-consumption rat race, the television as surrogate-parent and business relation as surrogate-friend culture? When these people begin awakening to their own non-identity and take fearful flight to escape it through alcohol, drug addiction, sexual profligacy, and even suicide—are these not to be numbered among the pathetically poor?

The material pauper and the emotional paralytic represent, of course, extremes in the category of need. But the point is both are impoverished and thus both have a claim on our concern. How vital it is, then, when examining our conscience, listening to a pulpit appeal for generosity in a poverty collection, or facing the other side across a bargaining table, that we see in reality it is not "them and us" but *We*. The circumstances of our individual conditions may vary, but the common material and spiritual requirements of our humanity join us, in Christ, as One.

Where need is concerned—whether our own or another's—Penance should help us to be frank with ourselves. Jesus promised that those who seek would find, and to those who knocked the door would be open (Lk 11:9). It is no sign of weakness or self-pity to allow our consciences freedom to uncover the particular needs we each have. There is truth to the old axioms that tell us God will not be outdone in generosity, nor will His grace be lacking for those whose needs are advanced in and through the whole community of faith.

Unlike the old "Strike it Rich" format where needy contestants were encouraged to vie for the "Heartline's" largesse by pitting the pathos of one's sob-story against another's, response to human concern in God's eyes is not a matter of adjudicating competing claims. The Lord of Love is no broker for the "separate peace" of individuals. His ordinary recourse to our prayerful appeals is not through miraculous relief for the few. More often than not the strength of God's grace we receive is supplied through the caring support shown us by those who have known similar need.

The saintly Mother Teresa of Calcutta tells of being visited by an Australian gentleman who was touched by just such empathetic grace. Having risen from an impoverished childhood to business success and wealth, the man came to Mother Teresa's Home for the Dying simply with the intention of offering a generous financial donation. But having written a substantial check he looked downcast and remarked to Mother, "That is something outside me, but I want to give something *of me.*" The next day he returned to the Home bringing with him a razor and shaving basin. He asked if he might take on the responsibility of coming regularly to bathe, shave, and talk to the terminally ill patients with whom he felt a real identity. Even great monetary generosity, he learned, could not substitute for sharing something of himself with those he found in need.**

A similar lesson was illustrated for this writer by a late personal friend. "Bill," only months before he died of cancer, arranged to fulfill a lifelong desire—a visit to Ireland, birthplace of his deceased parents. Like so many American tourists he hoped to locate distant relatives, or at least find natives who might recount for him something of his family's past. As dusk fell on a late-summer day Bill arrived in the small hillside village he believed closest to the vicinity of his ancestral homestead. Local farmers were beginning to gather in the town's pub for refreshment after a hard day in the fields. Bill entered and began introducing himself, hoping to find someone who might have knowledge of his family. Through the evening he chatted with villagers who passed through the pub, but no one he spoke to could recollect anything of his long-departed family.

Bill felt a growing sense of loneliness and disappointment as the evening wore on and his hopes remained unfulfilled. Finally, as he was about to give up sadly and leave the pub, an Irishman who had been standing at the bar and overheard his conversations asked if he might join Bill and treat him to a final round of ale. Bill accepted, though he asked of the stranger what prompted his hospitality. Smiling at Bill the man said softly, "Well, you're from America, aren't you?

** *Something Beautiful for God*, by Malcolm Muggeridge (1971, Harper & Row) p. 111.

And you've come a long way just to be in this place tonight. And you're searching for something here that's very important to you, am I right?" "Quite so," answered Bill. "Well come on have a drink, then," said the man. "Because, *you're one of us!*"

To be honest in admitting our own needs and sincerely seeking to "climb into the skin" of others to appreciate theirs is to enter into the process of peacemaking and reconciliation. For so many of our interpersonal and societal problems feed on the fearful myths and divisive tensions they foster among us. The deeper the anxieties we harbor about our own weaknesses, the more threatened we are likely to feel over the imagined strength and hostility of others. Thus in our culture, for example, the ghetto-dweller and the suburbanite have developed a serious antagonism. They are at odds in many respects (e.g. busing to achieve racial balance in schools, zoning, housing, welfare and taxation and equal opportunity legislation, etc.) and frequently resentful of each other. On the surface we might assume that no common bond of need exists between them. However, the more perceptive observer might notice that in many cases the apparent disdain each feels for the other's particular problems is generated by some degree of frustration at failure to cope with his own.

The predominantly lower-middle to lower economic income class ghetto-dweller, for instance, often knows precisely what's wrong in his life. He encounters daily tangible evidence of poverty, hunger, filth, degradation, danger, ignorance, disease, etc., yet remains largely powerless to effect remedies. He is well aware of how much he lacks financial and political "clout."

The suburbanite, on the other hand, may have the resources to do much, but finds it difficult to reduce many of his problems (marital differences, generation-gap strains, social and business pressures, nervous tension, etc.) to manageable or even definable terms. Under conditions where fears build easily and solutions come hard, those whose needs appear unlike mine—who "don't understand" my particular point of view—can loom all too temptingly as targets for the roiling aggression heated by impotence to control important affairs in my own sphere of life.

The Covenant of the Old Testament bound Israel to her God in faith. The New Covenant in the Blood of Christ binds each of us together in love. At every sacramental celebration we affirm that we are *wedded* to the community of belief that has inherited God's New Promise. The love that wedding seals is the unique hallmark of the Christian spiritual life. As a new Preface to the Nuptial Mass so beautifully expresses it:

> Love is man's origin,
> Love is his constant calling,
> Love is his fulfillment in heaven.

St. Paul glorifies marriage as the most powerful and intimate representation of Christ's love for His People, The Church (cf. Ep 5:29-32). The totality of giving, the unreserved commitment, the pledge of self-sacrifice on the other's behalf, and the witness to everlasting fidelity characteristic of sacramental marriage—all these are present in some degree to every other celebration of Christ's Presence as well. Our Baptism first introduced us to the ideal of Christian living. Confirmation fulfills our pursuit of that ideal. The Eucharist nourishes it. Penance restores us to it.

The Lord who makes his rain to fall "on good and bad alike" (Mt 5:45) invites us all to take each other "for better, for worse. . ." Jesus once replied to the sophistry of the Sadducees by declaring that in the Kingdom of Heaven there will be no marriage, such as we know it (Mt 22:30). One senses that he was not foretelling the *end* of a bond so magnificent in love and fidelity that it exhausts itself now in the union of only two. He was, perhaps, envisioning that day of boundless Love when the bonds now linking the few will be reforged to join all as One.

Chapter VIII

The Beatitudes - A Formula for Reconciliation

There is something of an anomaly about the Beatitudes. That litany of aphorisms that Matthew and Luke quote in substantially the same form (though for apparently different purposes) has provided grist for Scriptural scholars and spiritual commentators throughout the ages. At the same time the Beatitudes have never really seemed to have taken hold in the realm of popular spirituality as the *heavyweight* Gospel matter they were probably intended to be.

In Matthew's usage (5:1-12) the Beatitudes supply a script for a scenario that, in all likelihood, was designed to reveal Jesus as the New Moses. The Jewish audience to which Matthew appeals would have found significance in the deliberate parallels made with Old Testament lore. Like Moses on Sinai, the scene for the pronouncement of the Beatitudes (the "New Law") is set on a mountainside. The declaratory tone ("Blest are they who . . .!) strikes the note of authority the Jewish listener would associate with Mosaic utterances; the Beatitudes are arranged in Decalogue-like fashion; and like the Commandments the Beatitudes in Matthew call for a positive response from those who would enjoy God's blessing.

The Beatitudes in Matthew's Gospel serve as preamble to the extensive discourse in which Jesus pronounces a New Law ("You have heard it said . . . (but) what I say to you is . . .") designed to fulfill and thus supplant the Old. They are directive and hortatory.

The Beatitudes in Matthew have "third person" reference. ("Blest are *they who* . . ."). Those who achieve perfected development in the virtues mentioned are given acclaim. The usage is different in Luke. The second person is made the subject of address in the Lukan version ("Blest are *you* poor . . . hungry . . ., etc."), interpreting Jesus as reassuring those most deprived in this world that they will enjoy the greatest fulfillment in the Kingdom to come. In contrast to Matthew, Luke's Beatitudes are not so much a call to perfection as a pledge of God's special saving concern for those cast aside by the world. In addition, Luke also includes a parallel set of "woes"—passages warning the rich and complacent that the impending Day of Judgment will see them overthrown and crushed.

Scholars probing the ethical teaching of Jesus have wrestled with the meaning of the Beatitudes and over the years several interpretative theories have been advanced. Moral theologian Father Charles E. Curran notes that two of the most prominent have been the so-called "Moyses Moysissimus"—Moses to the nth degree—and "interim ethic" theories.** The former evolved from Lutheran theological roots and it sees the Beatitudes as impossible ideals beyond man's attainment in his sinful condition. Just as The Law forced Old Testament man to see his own weakness and corruption, the Beatitudes deliberately outline a moral program in the New Dispensation that man in his sinful condition cannot hope to live up to. The Beatitudes, this theory teaches, aim to disabuse the Christian of any pretensions toward salvation through (moral) works. Rather than set-

---

** "The Ethical Teaching of Jesus". *Commonweal,* vol. LXXXVII, no. 8, Nov. 24, 1967.

ting out to pursue the ideals that the Beatitudes hold out, man should acknowledge that sin makes it impossible for him to attain these ideals, and instead cast himself upon God's mercy "hoping against hope" for salvation through faith alone.

Albert Schweitzer was among the leading proponents of the "interim ethic" theory of the Beatitudes which gained some theological popularity around the turn of the century. This school believed that Jesus foresaw a relatively short period of time between his death and the coming of the *eschaton*—the Messianic Kingdom of God. He taught the Beatitudes, therefore, as short-term guidelines for Christian conduct; extremely demanding, yet bearable for believers who understood that relief from rigorous moral burdens was imminent. The power of God's Reign would soon over-shadow all.

Catholic tradition would find serious flaws in both the Moyses Moysissimus and interim ethic theories. The first seems to diminish Jesus as an authentic Teacher of moral values, and it does not allow for the presence of The Holy Spirit as Conveyor of those existential charisms supportive of moral living that we label "actual grace." Interim ethic seems to smack of a theological "cop-out." New Testament Scripture is simply too heavily weighted with evidence that Jesus conceived God's Reign as a reality *already present* to some extent among men. Christ's life appears largely devoted to teaching his disciples how to advance that Reign through lives given over to self-sacrificing, love-centered action. *Incarnation* is a doctrine instructing us that the Son was not a mere puppet lowered mechanically onto the stage of crea-tion to mouth a few pieties and then be whisked off again just ahead of an apocalyptic juggernaught called "The King-dom." We believe rather that the Lord Jesus "enfleshed" the world with His Body—the Community of His People—and breathed into that world His very Spirit, with long-range historical designs.

Since the Beatitudes constitute the "hard-core" of Jesus' moral discourse the various systematic theologies as well as the pastoral traditions of Catholicism have evolved frameworks of their own for understanding what the Beatitudes really mean in the day-to-day practice of Christian faith. Like the theories criticized above the tendency has been to deal with some of these "hard sayings" in somewhat compromising fashion. Father Curran offers this commentary:

> The Catholic theological tradition has generally ignored the problem created by the radical ethical demands of Jesus. At least on a popular level, Catholic teaching maintained that only a few people were called to perfection. Such people followed the evangelical counsels and generally entered the religious life. The vast majority of men living in the world were content with just observing the commandments which are binding on all men . . . Only with Vatican II does popular Catholic teaching stress the *universal vocation of all Christians to perfection* [italics mine.] **

Father Curran is not suggesting that the Church matter-of-factly taught such a dualist theory of morality as a part of Catholic belief. The Church's Teaching has always proclaimed that all persons baptized in Christ are bound to follow the challenging morality of the Cross. However, in practice the subtle tendency has been to translate the rigors of the *Gospel* mandate into those disciplinary features known to the mass of Catholics as fasting, abstinence, and "works of self-denial and mortification." When unsure about how the Catholic should go about transforming the world, we have found it a satisfying alternative to "push" passion-curbing reform of self.

** op. cit., p. 250.

Undeniably the Teaching Church in the post-Vatican II era has launched a hard-hitting new program for personal and communal moral initiatives against the alienating, dehumanizing evils of the time. There is a definite resurgence of zeal for the Gospel imperative as a basis for renewal in the everyday life of the Christian man and woman. The Beatitudes immediately recommend themselves as a blueprint for the kind of updated, life-affirming ethical spirituality especially suited to the Christian mission of healing and reconciliation. The Beatitudes make no distinction between "classes" of the faithful. They harbor no intimations about greater or lesser apostolic roles; no delusions about the depth of human suffering; no exemptions in their universal call to perfection. As the Gospels of Matthew and Luke bring these sayings of Jesus to us from complementary perspectives we see in them a wisdom that is at once practicable, empathetic and world-view inducing.

Since they summarize the essence of Christlike living in a form that makes for easy recall, the Beatitudes offer a particularly rich source of meditation or conscience examination matter for the maturing Christian. As we shall see, they readily lead us to questions about our attitudes and conduct that get right to the heart of what contemporary discipleship is all about.

Matthew's version opens with the famous, yet enigmatic line, "How blest are the poor in spirit." In assigning poverty of spirit to the pre-eminent place it occupies the Evangelist reveals that Jesus felt this virtue to be an underlying quality of life in God. Curiously, for such a vital factor in Gospel spirituality, a high percentage of otherwise "good Christians" seem unaware of what it means. Sermons are rarely preached on poverty of spirit, and few would include it on any list of most-highly-prized or eagerly pursued virtues.

Briefly, to be poor in spirit means to be *free*. It describes the person of faith sufficiently well-adjusted in personality and spirituality as to be above slavish dependence on the world's superficial marks of celebrity (status, power, wealth, etc.) for security or identity. Of course, simply being without material or social symbols of acceptance and success does not make one ipso facto poor in spirit. Poverty in spirit belongs only to those who show a clear sense of the Gospel priorities, and who value these above all else for their own sake. To be rich or poor by the world's standards does not of itself indicate the presence of spiritual poverty.

Exemplifying the kind of dedication in faith to the enrichment of others that characterizes real poverty of spirit is the figure of Mother Teresa whom we quoted above. In October 1974 news accounts reported that while Mother regularly accepts donations for her order's homes for the dying, leprosariums, orphanages and clinics, she once refused a check for $500,000 because it was intended as a "security fund" for her missionaries. Mother explained simply that so long as the poor have no such "security funds," neither could her sisters who identify with the poor accept such an endowment."**

Such poverty is also evident in the lives of those crusaders for social justice who have made the powerlessness of Jesus their own. In 1970 while battling the heavily financed forces of union-busting grape and lettuce growers, United Farm Workers organizer Cesar Chavez refused an impressive money grant attached to the annual Human Relations Award of the New York City-based Society for the Family of Man. In politely refusing the award Chavez wrote, "I have made it a policy not to accept such awards, in that the struggle is not mine, but that of thousands of farm workers."***

** National Catholic Reporter, October 25, 1974.
*** *Chavez: Man of The Migrants*, by Jean Pitrone. (1972, Alba House). p. 159.

To be free from the world's passions is to be free for the world's conversion. This, in sum, is the basis for the moral tone of Jesus in the Beatitudes. Unlike the Decalogue of Moses which aimed at setting limits ("Thou shalt not . . .") to human behavior in an effort to preserve man from infection by sin, the Beatitudes exemplify the encouragement Christ gives His followers to transcend those barriers sin erects to keep men divided and fearful. Those spiritually poor according to the world's standards are those who live unencumbered by the costly material and psychological weaponry designed only to dominate and destroy.

Those freely poor in spirit have the responsibility to make that same freedom available to others. For the human spirit to grow in dignity it must be cultivated in an atmosphere of human decency. Thus those poor in spirit for Christ should be in the forefront of the perpetual struggle against all forms of dehumanizing impoverishment. The first concern of Christ was always for the *anawim*—those wretched of the earth lacking in all but enslavement to poverty and oppression. Using as one of his first public forums the synagogue at Nazareth, Jesus rose and spoke out decisively about the earthly objectives of His Father's Reign. Making the ancient words of Isaiah his own, Jesus declared before that assembly:

> The Spirit of the Lord is upon me; therefore he has anointed me. He has sent me to bring glad tidings to the poor, to proclaim liberty to captives, recovery of sight to the blind and release to prisoners, to announce a year of favor from the Lord. (Lk 4:18-19)

Are we prepared to follow Jesus to that same rostrum? To endorse his "candidacy" as Lord and Savior? To make his "platform" our own? Perhaps some of those listening awestruck that day to the hard words of their "hometown boy" were moved deeply enough to become his lifelong followers. We *know* that most in that audience found him too much to bear, rushing forward as he concluded to hurl him from their midst. Can we bear hearing—dare we say *believing*—the echo of those terse phrases that, some heard him say, contain the words of eternal Life?

—BLESSED ARE THE LOWLY; THEY SHALL INHERIT THE LAND . . .

"It's not the earth the meek inherit, it's the dirt!" runs a line from the Broadway musical *Camelot*. Meekness carries with it a tone of enervation; a Caspar Milquetoast-like timidity as beneficial for survival in the hard-hitting competitive modern world as a humble prostration before a rumbling steamroller.

What Christ really praised in being "lowly" was neither material impoverishment nor servile abjection. The virtue actually being extolled here might best be described as honest *deference;* a sensitivity to the needs of others. Spiritual lowliness should not be equated with a psychological inferiority complex. Rather it is a mark of the balanced, secure person who has learned to discern and respect others' concerns as well as his own.

> Am I more in need of being 'ministered unto' than of ministering? Do I find myself often in need of impressing others with my talents and superiority? At home or on the job do I habitually put myself ahead of consideration for others? Do I find it hard to understand how others' needs or preferences can really be equal to or even greater than mine? What examples can I recall of showing sensitivity to the expressed *and* unexpressed needs of family or friends for my time? my concern? my willingness to listen? my support? my love?

—BLEST ARE THE SORROWING; THEY SHALL BE CONSOLED . . .

"Those who sow in tears shall reap rejoicing" the Old Testament claims. But is it really true that God has compassion for the suffering? After all, maybe *He's* the One Who brought it on in the first place—as a punishment for sin perhaps. And doesn't God seem furthest away in the moments of pain or tragedy? Maybe we suffer simply as a test of our faith?

There are probably as many theories on God and pain as there are sufferers in the world. Even those with the deepest faith—like Job the Arch-Sufferer of the Old Testament—find themselves speechless before the mystery. Yet some things we do know. For instance, as Christians we are not masochists. We do not seek sorrow for ourselves nor may we wish it on others. We do realize that suffering can enter our lives in ways and from sources totally beyond our control. Also we know that suffering will be an invariable result of our self-sacrifice, even as it was for Christ.

When the Lord Jesus blesses those who mourn it is with the promise of comfort that He does so. The heart's door is unlocked to sorrow and it can enter at any moment. We often have no say in the matter at all. Yet the decision *is* ours whether we will enclose that sorrow and hold it until it mellows into a joy at God's Peace with us in spite of all, or whether we choose to disgorge it as fast as we can through drains of bitterness, resentment, despair, or self-pity.

> Is my "hard day at the office" easily portable? Do I find it almost a matter of course that I take out my frustrations on others? Do I easily justify that extra after-hours "drink with the boys". . . that bit of back-biting over the fence . . . that heavy foot on the accelerator, as a tension or bitterness outlet? Have I let my pain convince me that God doesn't really care? Am I determined that whenever I suffer, by God I'll make sure someone else is just as uncomfortable!?

—BLEST ARE THEY WHO HUNGER AND THIRST FOR HOLINESS; THEY SHALL HAVE THEIR FILL . . .

In his inaugural address John F. Kennedy dedicated his administration to building a nation and world in which "the

strong are just, the weak secure, and the peace preserved."
That particular pursuit cost John Kennedy his life, and Dag
Hammarskjold his, and Martin Luther King his, and Jesus
Christ his. The annals of every nation's history record the
sacrifices of revered men, women, and children who valued
the good of many above any cost to themselves.

The Christian belongs in this world. He belongs in the
voting booth, at the PTA, the union meeting, the Kiwanis
luncheon, the picket line, even in jail—wherever ideas are
being floated or policies made that will affect the welfare of
a community.

Today on what environmentalist Buckminister Fuller
describes as our "spaceship earth" rapid transportation and
instant worldwide communications have made of our planet
a "global village." Significant developments in one area will
produce effects in all. Our responsibilities for contributing
to the decency and dignity of our world community are all
the more enhanced. Failure to care or to act for the greater
humanization of man anywhere will inevitably result in his
greater brutalization everywhere.

Pope Paul has said it bluntly but best: "If you want
Peace, work for Justice."**

> Am I an informed and active participant in the life
> of my neighborhood and community? Are my political
> and social views enlightened by the teachings of
> Christ and His Church? What steps am I taking to
> correct narrow-mindedness and prejudice in myself
> and others? Does my family see me as one "hungry
> and thirsty for justice"? If arrested on charges of being
> a Christian, would there be enough evidence to con-
> vict?

** Allocution proclaiming the *World Day of Peace*, January 1, 1972.

—BLEST ARE THEY WHO SHOW MERCY; MERCY SHALL BE
  THEIRS . . .

In the aftermath of the horrible kidnap-massacre of
Israeli athletes by Arab terrorists at the 1972 Olympic Games
in Munich, the grieving father of one of the innocent Jewish
victims was asked if he endorsed bloody Israeli reprisals
proposed in revenge for this tragedy. As a man with every
natural reason to call down blood upon others for his irrep-
arable loss, the father's response was remarkable in its nobility and conviction. "I want no such acts of revenge," he said.
"My son's life is its own lasting memorial, and that memorial
should not be sullied by a legacy of death."

It isn't all that hard to fall into a knee-jerk, tit-for-tat,
action-reaction pattern of living (or better, mere existence).
Saber-rattling, diplomacy-by-'brinkmanship' in international
relations, cutthroat sink-or-swim competitiveness in the business world, marital and family conditions (of the kind so
vividly dramatized in Edward Albee's *Who's Afraid of Vir-
ginia Woolf?*) where lines of communication fail and are
replaced by air-waves constantly filled with crackling elec-
tric tension—these all exist where the 'quality of mercy' has
been strained beyond all recognition.

Mercy is the handmaid of Hope. Patience, endurance,
and perseverance are all components of mercy and each
proves itself a showcase for our belief that sacrifice made for
the sake of good today will bear fruit in a better world tomorrow. To show mercy is to take the first step—the 'uncalled
for' step—to replace what has been shattered, rather than
cursing over ruins of beauty destroyed.

> Am I quick to devise subtle ways of punishing those
> who offend me? How deeply do I appreciate the toler-
> ance shown me by others when I offend them? When
> in the role of boss or disciplinarian are my actions
> guided more by a genuine concern for the best inter-

ests of others, or by a sense of self-aggrandizement? When was the last time I displayed mercy? the last time I consciously accepted an act of mercy from another?

—BLEST ARE THE SINGLE-HEARTED FOR THEY SHALL SEE GOD . . .

Man, Mark Twain once observed, is the only animal that blushes—or needs to. A variety of lessons might be drawn from that characteristically puckish statement. But most would boil down to the truism that our cheeks redden most when we're caught leading a "double life"—preaching or acknowledging the rectitude of one way of acting, while in fact doing quite another.

Single-heartedness (or purity of heart) is another of those key virtues that recur in the Gospel discourses of Jesus, but which are seldom the explicit subject of homilies or meditation. Basically single-heartedness calls on us to see our lives as Jesus saw his—rich in meaning and joy if consciously ordered to the Reign of God. Christ dares us to grab the plow and not look back, to face into the wind and steadfastly follow Him on the Way to glory.

All too often our tendency is to hedge our bets. We're willing to "render to God" one side of our spiritual coin, while reserving the right to retain the other. As St. Augustine self-critically analyzed the prayer of his early, unreformed life, "O Lord, make me pure and chaste—but not yet!"

> My conscious goals and ambitions in life—are they planned purely for my personal satisfaction, or with an eye to giving God glory and others help? Is my prayer life: (a) existent? (b) devoted exclusively to petitions and favor appeals? (c) rich in opportunities for weighing God's priorities against my own? Christian moral living—is it for me more a gamesmanlike way of *appeasing* God than a personal means for identifying with Him?

—BLEST ARE THE PEACEMAKERS; THEY SHALL BE CALLED SONS OF GOD . . .

> To wage war on misery and to struggle against injustice is to promote, along with improved conditions, the human and spiritual progress of all men and therefore the common good of humanity. Peace cannot be limited to a mere absence of war, the result of an ever precarious balance of forces. No, peace is something that is built up day after day, in the pursuit of an order intended by God, which implies a more perfect form of justice among men.
>
> —Pope Paul VI
> *On The Development of Peoples*

Renowned economist Barbara Ward, commenting on the encyclical of Pope Paul quoted above, observes that its chief note is one of "burning urgency." Indeed as we move rapidly toward the final quarter of man's least peaceful century there seems a spirit abroad—particularly among the young—to reclaim man from the final nuclear denouement that threatens to ring down the curtain on human civilization.

So much has war been a part of man's history that philosophers such as Thomas Hobbes in 17th Century England have concluded that strife is a constant in man's nature. The Christian rejects this reasoning, but must be prepared to admit that far greater sacrifices are necessary if the Church is to lead man toward all out peace. For as Pope Paul emphasizes, peace is an *active* virtue. It demands development of friendship and understanding, of equality in opportunity, of freedom and justice—beginning at wherever man calls home, and extending out to the world.

> If I *pray* for peace, am I willing to *work* for it? If world peace is my hope have I begun building it in my home, in my community? What commitments am I making of my hands, my heart, my pocketbook to support programs of peace-making development? Am I closer to pacificism or passivism?

—BLEST ARE THOSE PERSECUTED FOR HOLINESS' SAKE; THE
REIGN OF GOD IS THEIRS . . .

On several occasions Jesus is forced to rebuke his disciples for an overly exuberant fantasizing about the Kingdom to come, and particularly in regard to their imagined exalted roles in it. The Master is determined to leave his followers no doubts as to their abundant share in His sufferings. The message is the same for us. For if, as baptized Christians, we presume to reject the way of the world, then we had better full well realize that the world is quite prepared to reply to us in kind.

Our faith meets a stern test when caught up in what theologians call "eschatological tension"—that hard-to-reconcile awareness that God's Reign *has begun* in our midst, yet from all appearances the fullness of its coming in the hearts of all men must still be light-years away. There is no simple resolution to this stress-laden situation. Since the world is "groaning in agony" as it longs for reconciliation in God, the true Christian committed to a mission of healing in that world has no choice but to take its sufferings and make them his own. To be One with Christ means unity with His passion and death as well as Resurrection.

It is important, though, that we not forget the benediction the Lord Himself pronounces on those who suffer for His sake. The scars we bear are the unmistakable signs by which the Father recognizes us as brothers and sisters of His Son. It is to those who have sealed their love for God in the New Covenant of Christ's Blood that the Lord of Victory will address His singularly magnificent welcome: "Come, blessed of my Father, and take possession of the Kingdom prepared for you from the creation of the world!"

How willing am I to sacrifice popularity for principle? What evidence can I show to prove that I have taken others' sufferings as my own? What does the "sign of the cross" really mean to me?

Chapter IX

The Communal Personality of Penitent and Priest

Why should I have to confess my sins to the priest? Can't I just as well tell God directly and privately that I'm sorry? Why not simply have general absolution without going through the confessional routine?

Any priest will affirm that questions like these are among the first to be asked when discussion turns to the practice of Catholic faith today. Sometimes questioners are troubled by what they perceive as a trend away from frequent confession by an ever-increasing number of Catholics. Others are becoming more vocal in expressing dissatisfaction with the conventional confession-box procedure. Many apparently believe that drastically shortened Saturday confession lines together with developments such as communal penance services and the revamped Penitential Rite at the beginning of Mass augur a gradual "phasing out" of individual oral confession as we have it now.

A number of excellent books and articles have appeared recently which deal in depth with these concerns. Virtually all include strong pastoral assurances that person-to-person auricular confession ranks among the most hallowed of Christian traditions and will remain the ordinary means of entering into the Sacrament of Penance. Moreover the important new document on the revised *Rite of Penance*, while admitting the liceity of group absolution in special, extraordinary circumstances, stresses the need for renewal in the *personalist* dimension of the sacrament.

The main thrust of this document is toward enlightening the personal participants—the confessor and the penitent—as to the importance of their mission in the overall act of God's reconciliation with man. The new prescriptions call for a deeper human dialogue between priest and penitent, featuring shared prayer and Scripture reading, aimed at intensifying in both persons involved an awareness of the *ecclesial character* of what they are doing. Specifically, the document reminds the confessor that he must extend his ministry of reconciliation through preaching, personal example, and social action. He should bring to the Sacrament an acute feeling for the delicacy of a broken heart, the anxiety of a confused or sin-dulled conscience, the smoldering resentment of those denied care or justice. The penitent is reminded that he should bring to his confession a sense of what repentance involves in terms of his life in the community of man. Together they seek, in the context of the Sacrament, to grow in the mystery that is proclaimed in the new form for absolution:

> May God, the Father of mercies who by the death and resurrection of his son has reconciled the world to himself and poured forth the Holy Spirit, (now) through the ministry of the Church give you pardon and peace.* *

While the New Rite marks the first renewal of Penance in over 400 years, and comes at a time when the Church feels strongly in need of a reinvigorated spirit of repentance and conversion, the Sacrament's developmental history shows it to be one of the most powerful and adaptable media for the transmission of saving grace.

* * Quoted in "The Revised Rite of Penance", *Pastoral Life*, vol. XXIII, no. 4, April 1974.

The Gospels cite numerous examples of Jesus teaching and practicing forgiveness as a major part of His ministry. New Testament Scripture is also careful to note Christ's bestowal of "the power of the keys" upon His Church (cf. Jn 20:22-23; Mt 16:19, 18:18).

The formal administration of sacramental Penance in the early centuries of Christianity was apparently conducted under circumstances much different than what we are accustomed to today. Though members of the Christian community were urged to "confess your sins to one another, and pray for one another" (Jm 5:16), sacramental Penance was offered only to those who had sinned so grievously (i.e., by adultery, murder, or apostasy) as to warrant excommunication from the worshipping assembly. Following a lengthy period of public penance the penitent who had seriously violated his baptismal vows might be readmitted—but once— to fellowship in the faith community by the auspices of the presiding bishop.

Gradually the category of sinful offenses forgivable through resort to Penance became broader. By the fifth century it was common for the membership of the local churches to include an "order of penitents"—a special class of the faithful in process of atonement for serious sin, and preparing themselves for the reception of formal Penance.

Two elements are especially noteworthy about the practice of Penance in the early centuries of the Church. First, Penance was viewed in an ecclesial context. That is, the Sacrament was understood to reconcile the sinner once more with the community of believers in Christ—the Church. The early Christians held fast to their belief that the repository of saving grace lay within the visible body of the faithful. To be separated from that body was to be separated from God's love.

Second, Penance developed in the early Church from an

extraordinary means of reconciling the excommunicated few, to an ordinary sacramental channel for the perfection of the many devout. From the fifth through the tenth centuries Penance continued to grow in its availability to the people. It began to put off the image of a last resort from perdition, and take on the character of a salutary spiritual practice. With the rise of monasticism in the early Middle Ages the custom evolved among the faithful of visiting monks privately for confession and counseling. By the early 13th century Irish monks were compiling "penitential books" prescribing appropriate private penances for specific sins, and a form for absolution (*"Ego te absolvo..."*) was in widespread use. Pope Innocent III endorsed the frequenting of the Sacrament, and promulgated the following decree from the Fourth Lateran Council in 1215:

> Each member of the faithful of both sexes who has reached the age of discretion must confess his sins at least once a year to his own parish priest, and accomplish, within the measure of his means, the penance which is imposed . . .

Of course, the history of Penance includes many more details than we have sketched here. What matters most for our purposes is that from Pope Innocent's time to our own the Sacrament has assumed as its basic format a penitential dialogue between priest-confessor and penitent. That dialogue, we believe in faith, if conducted honestly, reverently, and thoughtfully, constitutes an encounter for both priest and penitent with the forgiving Christ.

The priest-confessor in Penance is the representative of Christ acting in and through His Church. It is not to Father Jones—isolated, random individual—to whom we confess, but to Father Jones, representative of those we have injured by our sins and with whom we seek reconciliation. It is not Father Smith acting on his own who grants us absolution.

It is Father Smith representing the authority of the Church empowered by Christ to forgive by whom we are absolved.

The privacy and the anonymity of the confessional box should not pre-empt the communal character of Penance. Though we need not undergo the public acts of penitence assigned to sinners in the early Church, it is still the whole community of God's People with whom we seek to be more completely reconciled through our participation in this Sacrament. Communal penance services and penitential liturgies should impress upon us the truly social extension both of sin and forgiveness. Every confession we make should be celebrated as the birth of New Peace between the Lord and ourselves; a Peace which must be carried out and shared with others.

The Sacrament of Penance is meant to be a Person-to-person encounter between Christ and ourselves through the ministry of His priest. Naturally, confession ought to be a reverent, sacred experience, but because it *is* a communication between persons it should be a relaxed, warm, and frank one as well. When reduced to a stylized exchange involving a perfunctory recitation by the penitent and "computerized" penance-cum-absolution formula from the priest both parties may suffer rather than benefit in spirit.

One reason, perhaps, why Penance has ceased to have any attraction for some and is approached only with great temerity by others, is the ultra-formalized, *juridical* character it may seem to them to have taken on. The Sacrament was never intended as a means for merchandising divine retribution. Its character of holiness derives from the opportunity it gives for renouncing the prideful sources of self-destruction and for regaining that precious sense of personal intimacy with the Lord so poetically idealized in Genesis as a "walk together . . . in the cool of the evening."

Surely there *is* a judgmental element in Penance. We

approach our confessor to acknowledge our personal responsibility for sin and to invite his corrective instructions and constructive advice. Still, along with an expanded appreciation for the communal aspect of Penance, we need (penitents and confessors alike) the makings of a more probative, cooperative confessional relationship. As theologians and contemporary commentators on Penance have noted, the model for our dealings with the priest in confession should be more one of physician-patient than judge-convict.

In the medieval days of the penitential books the task of the monk-confessor was to supply equitable punishment for the gravity of the matter confessed. The emphasis then was almost entirely on proper accountability and suitable reparation for misdeeds of the past. Confession then assumed the aura of a judicial arraignment.

With the more Scripturally-rooted appreciation we have for the Sacrament now, we realize that our future behavior must be considered if our Penance celebration is to be complete. It is especially important, then, that as we approach the Sacrament today we do so with the attitude that to help cope with the future confessor and penitent meet each other as collaborators in a common cause. Their mutual goal is the perfection of the penitent's ability to live the Gospel message and to spread it most effectively.

As "Father" in the confessional, the priest must be able to set the proper sacramental mood. The penitent should sense in his confessor a prayerful sense of rejoicing at contrition and conversion. The good confessor sees himself as a receiver of man in his sinful incompleteness. His responsibilities in the confessional do not include formal psychiatric therapy, yet the priest today should work to develop insights that will help, in gentle conversation, to bring out of the penitent the real truth about his needs and weaknesses. The confessor should always bear in mind that his unique role involves *walking with* the penitent; facing together with him the great mysteries of evil and grace. Many of the problems penitent and confessor confront together demand patience and faith in both. Marital and family difficulties, sexual anxieties, social adjustment hardships, emotional imbalance, alcoholism—these are some of the critical wounds afflicting the human spirit that call for "medication" in the form of encouragement, support and understanding from the confessor. "Right answers," quick or easy solutions may well be out of the question. It is up to the confessor to show the kind of humility in the face of mystery that marks genuine spiritual leadership. It is not to spew out computerized answers that the priest sits in the confessional, but to *pray*—for and with the penitent. *Real prayer*, that is, not sanctimonious mumbo-jumbo. With the fearful he must speak the words of Hope: behold, I am with you all days! With the depressed or despairing he must show himself a follower of the compassionate High Priest; capable of understanding and eager to reconcile. To those encrusted with bitterness or prejudices the confessor must wield the "two-edged sword" with surgical precision: speaking candidly of the Lord's esteem for all mankind, while coaxing the penitent to see himself as a joy-filled new man in Christ—free and at peace when willing to call each of his neighbors "brother." Most of all, the priest should see something of himself in all who confide their sins and hurts in him. The confessor is not ordained to pass judgment on the failings of lesser mortals. Conscious of his own need for reconciliation, he should make the appeal of every sinner for forgiveness his own. Extending his arms in the sign of absolution he is most a sacrament of the crucified Lord when he sees himself—and the penitent knows him to be—what writer Henri Nouwen so touchingly describes as the "wounded healer."

A word to those who question the necessity or efficacy

of confessing to a "mere man." First, let us remember that our less-than-serious sins can be forgiven in a variety of ways outside of formal confession: e.g., participation in the Eucharist, prayer, and surely through those acts we perform to rectify and atone for the wrongs we have done. At the same time it is vital that we see Penance as an integral part of a sacramental system designed to bring us in touch with the living, Personal Presence of Christ. Again, that uniquely Christian doctrine of the Incarnation informs us that it is through human Personhood that God chooses to reveal Himself most completely. It follows then that the Sacraments, the visible signs of the Lord's ever-Present care for us, ought to be occasions when God's People share most profoundly in the communal, the interpersonal modes of exchange reserved exclusively for contact between God and man.

Archbishop Sheen tells the story of a woman who questioned him about the necessity of prayer. Does your husband love you? he asked. Of course! she replied. Has he ever told you he loves you? Certainly! she said. With a twinkle in his eye the Archbishop commented, "only *once?*" The point is that the fully human feeling needs a fully human, external expression that needs to be verbalized or acted out repeatedly. Confession is our moment to unburden ourselves openly to Christ; to hear ourselves renounce the evil we have done; to feel the weight of our sins transferred to His waiting shoulders. In return ours is the privilege of *hearing* what Zacchaeus, and Mary Magdalene, and the Prodigal Son of the parable rejoiced to hear for themselves: "Your sins are forgiven!"

As a concluding postscript, we might consider for one moment something that seems so necessary yet so often lacking among so many of us. That is a sense of *gratitude*—an attitude of appreciation for what the Lord fashions for us in the Signs of His Church. Understandably, sweeping renewal within the Church and swirling currents of social and political change have given many the opportunity to drift away from—or at least question—the more traditional practices of their earlier religious life. We must not be quick to condemn those who are honestly searching for new authenticity in their relationship with God.

Yet in the midst of so many pretensions to "activity" there seems to be a decay in religious practice that amounts to nothing more than apathy. Any number of excuses can be unearthed to rationalize abandonment of the Sacrament of Penance. As we have sought to emphasize throughout this book, real *effort* is required in the quest for reconciliation; plentiful and patient effort to develop a deep-probing examination of conscience; to plan and execute future-oriented strategies for life-style changes; real effort to find work with, and learn to relate well with a Christlike confessor. Measured exclusively on this scale, the price of forgiveness through Penance may indeed seem high.

For that price—whatever it may be for us personally— we are entitled to a few moments of quiet conversation with a man of God. He whispers at last the simple words of the formula stating that by the authority of the Risen Lord Jesus Christ, One in the Father of mercies and Holy Spirit of Life, ". . . I forgive your sins."

How many down through the ages would have surrendered all their riches to hear those words spoken to *them* and be able to believe what they say? How many who have knelt on hillsides and shrieked to God for mercy have heard in reply only the mindless beating of the wind? How many would have paid the highest price many times over for but one opportunity at what is available to us as routine?

> I tell you solemnly, many prophets and holy men longed to see what you see, and never saw it; to hear what you hear, and never heard it. (Mt 13:17)